ENOUGH ALREADY

Create Success on Your Own Terms

MIKE IAMELE

Conari Press

First published in 2015 by Conari Press, an imprint of
Red Wheel/Weiser, LLC

With offices at:
665 Third Street, Suite 400
San Francisco, CA 94107
www.redwheelweiser.com

ISBN: 978-1-57324-647-7

Library of Congress Cataloging-in-Publication Data available upon
request

Cover design by Jim Warner
Cover images: fish © Kudryashka / shutterstock,
legs © tack tack / shutterstock
Interior by Maureen Forys, Happenstance Type-O-Rama
Typeset in Adobe Garamond Pro and Gotham

Printed in the United States of America.
EBM

10   9   8   7   6   5   4   3   2   1

To my **Bubbie** for teaching me how to dance.

To **AJ** for teaching me how to laugh.

To my **family** for teaching me how to support one another.

And to **Garrett** for teaching me how to love.

I am forever grateful for a journey filled with dancing, laughter, support, and love. To me, that is success.

CONTENTS

EVERYONE HAS A STORY (AN INTRODUCTION OF SORTS)

When I was twenty-two, I thought I was really successful. I can even pinpoint this feeling to a specific night. It was the Boston premiere of *The Social Network*, and I had tickets.

I was weeks away from finishing my last semester of college. I had just endured a long day of classes in the morning and eight hours of work in the afternoon. Not a college job. Not an internship. Real work. I had helped to start a PR agency only a few months before. And, in just a few weeks, I'd be graduating to take on my rightful spot as part owner.

I was an expert on healthcare technology and healthcare reform. My résumé had been sent to the White House twice. I worked with big-name, national reporters. I had more than enough money. And friends. Plenty of friends.

There I was, waiting for the premiere of a movie to start. I was successful. I was important. I mattered.

But, as the movie started to roll, playing out the story of Facebook's impressive founding, I couldn't help but think that maybe my life was more filled with carefully crafted credentials and glossy photos than anything else.

And, looking at my friends to my left and right, I started to suspect that I wasn't the only one.

Beginnings are awkward. I never know where to start. Whenever I have no clue how to begin something, I try to think about whatever I'm doing like a little kid would.

Have you spent much time around children? They approach everything with a little naïvety, a heavy dose of curiosity, maybe a splash of wonder—and the annoyingly persistent question: "Why?"

Us adults, we gave up on our questioning years ago. Things just are. We accept them and move on. We don't have time to sit around and philosophize. We're off working long hours and paying the bills and doing chores and just trying to survive everyday life.

But now we're in a predicament because I already said that I'm approaching this just like a kid would. And you're reading a book about success. So I'm going to guess that you care about being successful, at least a little bit.

So I've got to ask: Why? Why do you want to be successful?

I've asked this question more times than I can remember. In fact, I ask this question when I first meet with any client. And, every single time, I get the exact same response: a blank stare. That's not entirely true. Once, someone asked how I made it this far in my business asking stupid questions like that.

But I don't think it's a totally unfair question. I mean, success is the end-goal for the vast majority of people. It comes up in casual conversation every day. And let's face it—Facebook has become little more than a gauge on how successful people have become since high school.

Our heroes have changed from actors and athletes to Mark Zuckerberg and Sean Parker. Our culture values the ideal of achieving astronomical success at a young age over almost anything else. We're a culture obsessed with success. All I'm asking is why.

Okay, I'll go first. If I'm being honest, I wanted to be successful for all the reasons you're not supposed to want it. Because it'd make me matter. It'd make me important. The cars, the chicks, the whole bit.

I was sold a fairy tale of success, and I bought it—hook, line, and sinker. I grew up believing that I'd work my little butt off, put in my time, pay my dues, and be rewarded with the pot at the end of the rainbow. I'd have money, fame, and power. My name would mean something.

I wanted to cover myself with fancy parties, impressive job titles, and large salaries because I was afraid that if people peeled back the layers, they wouldn't like what they found. Underneath, I wasn't enough. Not rich enough or smart enough or charming enough or experienced enough or old enough or good enough.

I was convinced that, once I made it "there," things would be different. People would look at me differently, treat me differently. Hell, I'd treat me differently.

I wouldn't let people walk all over me anymore. I wouldn't waste time on things that didn't make me happy. I'd have honest relationships. I'd have time for myself. Success would get me everything I wanted.

Turns out, I was confusing success with self-esteem. And, if I didn't have it from the get-go, no arbitrary milestone of "success" was going to bring self-esteem along.

This book in your hands lays out the journey I took to success. How I gave up looking for external validation and started building internal worth. How I rejected society's definition and started defining success as what would make me happy. How I recovered from a serious illness and stopped burning myself out. And, most of all, how I started helping people across the world create success on their own terms.

This book is set up like a journey—a hero's journey, to be exact. It's split into twelve chapters, or stages, of the journey. Each chapter begins with a short story from my own life, followed by an in-depth discussion of the topic at hand, and finally ends with a few challenges to help you incorporate that step into your life.

But I need your help. The book is incomplete without you. I can only give you the framework; you've got to fill in the picture. If you choose to complete the challenges and follow the steps in order, you'll have created a personalized guidebook for your own path to success. Not for the life somebody else envisioned for you, but for the life you've always secretly wanted.

When I first started writing this book, I thought I'd just be sharing some wisdom from my journey. I thought that I'd be plotting out the map, pointing out the sights, sharing the tour guide's insider scoop. But, somewhere in the process of writing it, I was forced to take a hard look at myself. I was forced to answer the tough questions: *Am I actually successful? What does that mean to me? Am I completely happy? Where could my life be better?*

And I found myself—the expert, the writer, the guide—smack dab in the middle of yet another success journey. Doe-eyed and ambitious, I entered each step with more guts and glory than the one before. And I was spit out the other end of this book with the realization that I can be more successful than I ever knew was possible. Take it from the guy who's written the book on success: we're always cycling through deeper and deeper levels of success. No matter where you are in your journey, or how many times you've circled it, I hope this book can work it's magic on you, just like it has on me.

But, before we go on, I have a rule—just one rule—for anyone reading this book. It's my number one rule in my practice, and I feel like I'd be a hypocrite if I didn't lay down the law here: we don't measure magnitude; we measure direction. It doesn't really matter if you leap or skip. Doesn't matter if you tiptoe or crawl. All that matters is that you move. That you move in the direction of your goals.

This isn't another self-help book to lay untouched on your bookshelf. This isn't just another inspirational story.

If you want to reach success—real success—you can't read and think about it all day. You have to move. You have to take the challenges and do something with them. It doesn't matter if you do every challenge or just one per chapter—just that you do something. Because if you take one tiny step every day toward your goals, at the end of a year, you'll be 365 times closer to accomplishing your dreams.

Beginnings are awkward because they require trust. They require you to let go of your fears and anxieties and cynicism and insecurities. They require you to blindly take a step forward and watch the path develop as you go. They require you to start before you're ready.

So, enough already. It's time to start.

1

You Can't Get Started if You Don't Know Where You're Going

I'd always assumed I'd be successful. Not in an arrogant way. Not even in a hopeful way. It just kind of made sense. Like how I assumed I'd graduate high school.

I did everything right. I got the right grades. I got into the right schools. I joined the right clubs. Got the right internships. Networked with the right people. Climbed the right ladders.

To the outside world, I'd made it by my mid-twenties. I had a job I loved that paid me a lot of money. I had a gorgeous apartment, invitations to parties across the city, a booming social life, *and* I was working on stuff that mattered. I wasn't just making money for money's sake. I was working in healthcare reform, politics, cutting-edge technology, and medical research.

I did it right. I did everything right. I was successful by all accounts. But success didn't really feel like success.

It felt like . . . blood. All over my bathroom floor.

It was the middle of the summer, and I woke up one morning after a night of drinking. *Hangovers are the worst*, I told myself. But they usually didn't involve vomiting blood.

Three days later, the blood didn't stop. I was rushed to the hospital. No one had any idea what was wrong with me. I was bent over in pain, vomiting massive amounts of blood. And it wasn't slowing down.

Suddenly, the corporate climbing didn't seem so important. The meaningful job didn't feel so meaningful. And I desperately clung on to the hope that my life would amount to more than a brief encounter with workaholism.

I gave up on success. I totally and completely gave up on success—at least the version that I knew. I had played my cards exactly right. But all it got me was sick, stressed, and unhappy.

Crying in an emergency room bed, as doctors rushed to find out what was wrong with me, I made a decision—one that would change my life. I decided to stop buying into someone else's story of success.

And I started writing my own.

Every Crisis Is an Opportunity

We're in the middle of a success crisis. Students are graduating from college with no career opportunities in sight. Seasoned business veterans are being replaced by younger, cheaper talent. People are climbing to the top of the corporate ladder and realizing they may have gotten on the wrong ladder. Others are starting their own endeavors, only to be swimming in an endless ocean of anxiety and workaholism. No matter what we do, it seems like we can never find fulfilling success.

Forget about midlife crises, we're having quarter-life crises. The traditional roads to success have dried up. With corporate downsizing and layoffs, we can no longer rely on the conventional résumé-building approach. There simply isn't the same job security to build a long-term career. On the other hand, opportunities for success are accessible to the general public like never before. In the age of telecommuting and social media, anyone with a laptop can start a thriving company.

We have endless possibilities laid out before us, and we're paralyzed. Because, to take advantage of them, we have to decide what we really *want*. We're in the driver's seat. We can no longer follow someone else's model for success. We can no longer copy someone else's approach. We've tried that already, and it's left us all burnt out and miserable. Today, the only way to find lasting and fulfilling success is to define it for yourself.

In the modern era, we've broken the business model and disrupted the industry so many times that there's no clear-cut example for how to do things anymore. Billion-dollar corporations started in garages. High-end executives are dropping the million-dollar salaries for a simpler life. Kids are becoming famous from posting videos on YouTube. Success is whatever you decide it is today.

Even the currency of success has changed. Money, power, and recognition are no longer the only paper bills in the game. What about time? Or relaxation? Or corporate culture? Or meaningful contribution to the world?

In today's world, success has many currencies. People are leaving high-powered jobs to buy more free time in their lives. They're taking pay cuts just to experience better workplace atmosphere. They're dropping out of the rat race and volunteering for purpose-driven companies.

Success can be bought with whatever currency is most important to you. At its root, success is really about what will bring you to happiness. And, if money isn't the only wealth that can bring you there, you need to start investing in something else.

If dropping out of the workforce to stay home with kids is important to you, I'd call that success. If getting to spend more time on the golf course matters to you, then maybe it's worth taking the pay cut. The point is that success is whatever we define it as.

The idea of a "job" is falling by the wayside. People are working on several projects with multiple revenue streams. They're turning products into services and services into products. They're intersecting industries and mish-mashing business models. Mostly, they're doing things on their own terms.

Working eight-hour days might be for you. But working around-the-clock with periodic breaks could be more your style. Or maybe you like saving up and then taking a month vacation every few years. Or even traveling the world while you're working.

Success can really be anything you want, but you just have to define what that is. In theory, it's simple. In practice, it's damn near impossible.

If it were that easy, a whole lot more of us would have what we wanted today—or at least have direction on how to get it. We have enough trouble picking out a movie to watch on Netflix. But knowing what we want to do with our lives? That's a mighty tall order.

It's not enough to pick a job in the right field. Do you work for someone or go your own way? What kind of corporate culture are you looking for? What kind of boss could you stand working for? How many hours would you like to work? What kind of pay would you demand? How much stress could you handle?

The questions start piling up. The analysis paralysis shifts into high gear. And we're tempted to follow somebody else's example, rather than start from scratch ourselves.

But, if we're going to create success on our own terms, we have to throw out the old success equation. We have to rip up that old map. It's the Wild Wild West. If you want to find success for yourself, you're going to have to venture into uncharted territory. You're going to have to draw up a new map from scratch. You're going to have to answer the age-old question: *What does success mean to you?*

Success Feels Natural

The good news is you probably already know what it looks like and just don't realize it.

Let's look at an example. When do you feel more successful? When you're in a suit presenting to a room full of judging clients? Or when you're laughing along with friends?

The first step to deciding what success looks like to you is actually letting go of what you want it to look like (or, at least, what you think you want), and starting to embrace what it already does look like.

We're so inundated with the wants of our friends or family or bosses or significant others that it's hard to tell what we actually want anymore. We feel like we're *supposed* to be a certain way or do a certain thing. We play a part, we fit a role, we make ourselves into the perfect little package of who we think we should be. And we so badly want to be that person.

We have so many rules for a successful life: promotion by age twenty-five, marriage by thirty, make partner by thirty-five. We continuously compare ourselves to everyone around us. We check how we stack up to society's timeline. We surround ourselves with *have-tos* and *shoulds* of the lives we think we're supposed to live.

Instead of wishing you were some specific version of success, let's figure out when you feel most successful already. I mean, you're probably already pretty successful in some ways. So why not use those as examples?

Maybe you have good friends with whom you love hanging out. Or maybe you have a really successful romantic relationship. Or just a good connection with your boss. Or a mom you call once a week. Or a client that you secretly counsel on life.

The thing all of these *successful* situations have in common is that they've required relatively little effort to cultivate. You probably don't even really feel like you're trying. You're just doing your own thing, being yourself, and—*bam!*—you've created a successful situation.

We know what success feels like. We *all* know what success feels like already. It feels like laughing with friends or playing a board game with family or staying in on a Friday night to watch your favorite movie. It's fun, it's easy, and it makes you happy.

Success feels natural to us. It plays to our strengths; it comes really easily; it's so much fun that we could do it all day; and it always happens when we're so lost in our passions that we forget to try. Success is about creating a life that's easy and enjoyable for you. It's about doing what you love every single day. And it's really hard to get burnt out if that's the way you live your life.

But, when we're following somebody else's model for success, we start following their rules. We push ourselves to be just like them. And then we end up working really hard at something that just doesn't come naturally to us.

You never have to try to be yourself. If you're trying, it means you're being somebody else.

So, the first step to unlocking your own definition of success is just letting go of what you want success to look like, and starting to think about the way it already looks in your life. As you start to pick apart the successful parts of your life, you're well on your way to figuring out what success looks like to you.

Success Feels Big

Now, going to the bathroom every day may feel natural, but few people would regard that as overwhelming success. If you felt that your life was already successful as it is, you wouldn't be reading this book. So, in addition to natural, we need success to feel big. It always feels big. It has to— otherwise you're not challenging yourself. And we never feel successful when we're in our comfort zones. We feel complacent, bored, content, cozy—but never successful. Success comes when we expand beyond ourselves, when we show ourselves that we can be bigger than we imagined.

Your definition of success, whatever it is, has to scare you. Even just a little bit. It has to feel bigger than you've imagined yourself before—whether that means living on an exotic beach or just taking an occasional lunch break with friends. It has to feel like growth. In fact, part of success is constant growth. We're hard-wired to keep expanding. We have an intrinsic need to push past our boundaries and continue growing. Any attempt to stay in your comfort zone is just going against biology. No wonder we have so many mid-life crises.

Something happens when things are scary—something big. Our eyes widen, our hands get jittery, and our hearts start to race. We call it nervous excitement. I've always liked that phrase *nervous excitement*. Because it's nervousness or excitement; it just depends on how you look at it. That same feeling of anxiety is what flips on the nerves in excitement too. It's what brings our bodies into action mode. It's what brings life back into us.

Some people backpack the world, or buy a Ferrari, or even take drugs to feel that nervous excitement we so badly crave. I personally prefer to live a successful life.

Success feels big and exciting because we have to lay all the cards out on the table. We have to be really vulnerable and own up to all the things we actually want. It doesn't matter if we don't feel good enough, or we don't think it's possible, or we don't feel ready. Success isn't about our limiting beliefs, it's about our deepest desires. It's about designing a life that's never been lived before. And, boy, does that take guts.

When we start growing big—really, really big—we do things we never thought in a million years that we could do. We dare to dream. We act like kids again. We imagine impossible things and then try to do them anyway, just for fun. We dig up those buried desires. We let ourselves want what we want. We forget our favorite excuse: "I can't." We try things even if we're not sure we're going to succeed.

To ever reach success, you have to give up knowing for sure that you'll ever get there. You have to stop doing the things that you know you'll succeed in. Success is about taking a gamble. It's about betting it all. It's about putting all your money on yourself because you know that you're worth it.

If you can dream up a life that big and scary, then success is just within your reach.

Success Feels Nourishing

I don't think anybody's definition of success ever started with, "I want to work eighty hours a week and hardly ever sleep." But that's exactly what society has been telling us that success means. It's a rat race. We're told to either achieve success *or* take care of ourselves. Not both at the same time.

But success—or, at least, any sustainable version of it— has got to include some nourishment. It can't be all give and no take. Success is a relationship. And, like any healthy relationship, we've got to get back just as much as we give. We've got to be strengthened, supported, and energized by the very thing we're creating. Otherwise, we're going to tire out real quick. And that just leads to burnout and resentment.

Think of the things that enliven you. The things that you could stay up all night doing—talking to friends, writing poetry, arguing about healthcare reform, playing videogames. All of these things provide some form of nourishment. You may come home from work completely exhausted, but then someone recommends a game of Frisbee, and you're immediately refreshed. Any activity that's worth making it into your definition of success has got to nourish you to the core.

Remember, we're not doing the success thing five days a week and hanging up the Superman cape the other two. We're not just trying to build successful careers here; we're trying to build successful lives. We finally acknowledge that we're not just compartmentalized robots. Personal life affects work life, and vice versa. Our relationships are just as important to our success as our career impact. So we need to be nourished by whatever it is that we choose to do with our lives. We need to get really clear on what it is that makes us feel alive and then plow forward with that.

If you can define success as the thing that brightens your spirits and nourishes your soul, you'll never have trouble getting out of bed to do that.

You Are the Judge of Your Own Success

It sounds good. It sounds inspirational. But just living a life that's natural, big, and nourishing isn't necessarily successful, is it? I mean, that could define anything from a fisherman in a small village to a stay-at-home parent to a high-end executive. Are all these people really equally successful?

If we're going to create success on our own terms, then we're going to have to take back our power to define it. Corporate America has commandeered success for far too long, and we've been beaten over the head with its definition of a high-powered job and large salary. Maybe that's your definition of success, maybe it's not. But, if you don't define it for yourself, you'll never be happy when you achieve it. Because it's never what you wanted in the first place.

Even natural, big, and nourishing are just guidelines to get you started. If they don't feel right to you, trade them in for ones that do. Success can be anything from changing healthcare to following your passion to raising a beautiful family. You get to decide what success means to you.

The sky's the limit, and only you know what you really, really want underneath. So don't be afraid to think up your absolute ideal. Remember, we're only in the defining stages right now. It doesn't matter if it seems impractical or impossible. It doesn't matter if it changes throughout this book or throughout your life—it probably will. That's the nature of success. It's always changing because you're always changing. But all that matters right now is that you're being honest with yourself and allowing yourself to want what you really want.

Nobody can tell you if you're successful or not. Nobody can judge how successful you are. You're playing by different rules than everyone else. You're going by different definitions of success. And your version of success is just the journey that's going to bring you to happiness. So you need to decide what will take you there.

Your definition of success is your blueprint, your strategy plan, your roadmap to get you where you want to go. You've already laid out the main points on the path. You've already described how you want it to look, feel, taste, smell, and sound. Now all you have to do is follow along the journey.

When you know where you're going, you know how to get there.

CHALLENGES

Complete the following challenges before moving on to the next chapter. I recommend reading them all over before you decide which ones to do. You can do all of them, some of them, or just one, but you have to do something. If you want to create success for yourself, you have to define what it is you're trying to create from the get-go.

1. Spend some time thinking about the success you want to create in the future. Take out a pen and piece of paper and write the first things that come to mind when you read the following questions:

    I.   What does success mean to me? What does it look like? Feel like? Sound like? Smell like? Even taste like?

    II. How much money do I make when I'm successful? How important is money? What do my relationships look like? What do my friendships look like? What kinds of foods do I eat? How does exercise fit into my life (if at all)? What kind of luxuries do I enjoy?

    III. How do I let people treat me? How do I treat myself? What do I accomplish in the world? How much free time do I have? How do I value my time?

    IV. What is it about my life that makes me feel most successful?

2. Think about the most successful aspects of your life right now—whether they are relationships, work, a particular card game, or family time. Write down what all of these aspects have in common. What is it about them that makes them all successful?

   I. Now write down what other skills come naturally to you. Maybe you're a great writer, or a good listener, or a whiz on the computer. Write down whatever naturally works for you.

   II. Your fastest route to success is leaning on the skills that are already successful in your life right now.

3. Think about your biggest dreams—the stuff that seems way out of your reach. Maybe you're being interviewed by Oprah. Maybe you just bought that gorgeous condo in Hawaii. Maybe you've impacted millions of lives. Whatever your dreams, write down the ones that feel the biggest and scariest. These are the ones that matter most to you, and the ones that you define as successful. Some aspect of these dreams needs to be part of your success definition.

4. Notice the activities that seem to give you the most energy. Maybe it's going to the opera or playing a game of basketball. Maybe it's journaling in the morning or passionately arguing about politics. Whatever gives you energy and makes you feel strong is something

that nourishes you. Write down the activities that most nourish you, and that you feel like you could do for hours on end.

5. Give yourself permission to create success on your own terms. Right here, right now decide to give up the way others have defined success for you and decide to define it for yourself. Write out one paragraph about what success means to you. This will be your roadmap to create success on your own terms.

2

Every Journey Needs a Compass

Tears streamed down my face. I was an adult—twenty-four years old—trapped in the bathroom at my office. I couldn't even bring myself to look at my reflection. I had an accident at work. I could no longer control my bowels. My sickness had worsened.

My hand shook nervously as I texted the office manager to put an "out of order" sign on the bathroom door. I texted a colleague to pack up my stuff and bring me a change of clothes. I was sneaking out the back entrance. I had hit the lowest of the low.

I was scheduled to go in for an MRI about two weeks out. Doctors had determined that I had severe pancreatitis, which had been undiagnosed for a while. I also had infections in four major organs. There could have been more. There probably was more.

The question wasn't how sick I was; it was how permanent the damage would be. My pancreas looked in bad shape.

There's a certain freedom in hitting rock bottom. When people see you at your weakest, your embarrassment threshold is far greater. Any attachment I had to my previously "successful" identity had withered fast. I didn't care about how silly or stupid I looked; I just wanted to get better.

With my newfound sense of freedom, I began my wellness blitz. I found myself trying things I'd never have imagined with practitioners I'd previously referred to as quacks. Every day was something new: acupuncture, meditation, reflexology, Reiki. Letters forgiving anyone who ever wronged me. Letters apologizing to anyone I ever wronged. I wrote painfully honest emails to family members. I read uplifting stories. I treated myself to romantic date nights. I changed my diet. I changed my thoughts more. I let myself laugh. I let myself cry.

And, two weeks later, as I went in to find out the damage to my pancreas, I didn't need a test to tell me what I already knew. I was better. Not just a little bit. Not just in less pain. Better. The MRI showed no sign of disease.

As I walked out of the doctor's office with a smile on my face, I caught my own reflection in the mirror. I wasn't the same person who had walked into that office just a few months before.

I was no longer afraid.

We All Need a Little Direction Sometimes

Being a pioneer is tough. Without somebody else's map to follow, you have to navigate uncharted territory. There are no coordinates to copy or rules to guide you.

But all good pioneers, from Christopher Columbus to Davy Crockett, had at least one tool in their bag of tricks. They had one gadget to let them know if they were on the trail or missing the mark: a compass.

If we've thrown out the prevailing success map and created our own, then we're all pioneers ourselves. This is new terrain, and we've got to chart a new path. Just like all of the explorers and adventurers before us, we're going to need something to guide us through. We're going to need a compass.

Fortunately, the human body is equipped with a trusty compass of its own: emotions. And there's one emotion that time and time again can spot out an opportunity for success. One emotion that, hands down, always points us in the direction of our dreams. One emotion that tells us exactly where we need to go to keep moving forward. *Fear.*

I think we can all agree that we don't like being afraid. We pretty much avoid the things we fear at all costs. We make excuses, we run away, we pretend that it doesn't really matter to us. Because it's easier to give up on our dreams than it is to face our fears.

But the truth is that you wouldn't feel something as intense as fear if it weren't important to you. Fear doesn't just point out the important stuff, it points out just how important the stuff is. The more afraid you are, the more important it is to you.

See, we shy away from the things we fear, not because they aren't important to us, but because we don't think we're good enough for them. We're terrified that, if we finally get a chance to step up to the plate, we might completely whiff. All of our limiting beliefs will become realities. And that's something we can't handle. So we take ourselves out of the race. Because at least then we have an excuse for never winning.

But, if we were really honest with ourselves, we'd admit that the things we fear are the exact hurdles we have to overcome to get where we want to be. They're the "standing up to your boss" and "finally opening that restaurant." They're the "moving across the country" and "finally asking that person out." They're the things standing between where we are and where we could be.

Without fail, fear will always point you in the direction of due north. And what you're most afraid of is always the next hill that you have to overcome.

Trace Your Fears Back to the Start, Ugly Duckling

The first step to moving past your fears is to see where they came from in the first place. Our fears all come from somewhere—maybe an offhand comment our mom made about our weight, or that time school kids made fun of our stutter. Whatever it was, it scarred us for life, and now we've learned that we're not safe to be that exposed again.

Wait, what?! We're holding ourselves back from success now because of something that happened long ago? We're really afraid to live the lives we want because of a failure or pain that happened once before?

You're living in an adult's body with a child's fears. Even if the source of the fear is relatively fresh, you've come a long way since then. Every experience, every moment is helping us to grow. And you aren't the same person that you used to be. You aren't even the same person that you were five minutes ago. Not by a long shot.

Wake up and check your reflection, ugly ducking. You've blossomed into a swan.

So many of us are afraid to re-check our reflections. We're afraid of trying our failure again, or revisiting that past hurt, or exposing ourselves to vulnerability. But if the duckling never checked his reflection, he'd never have known he became a swan.

You've come a long way from where you were. Whatever happened in the past can stay there. You're a different person. You have different skills. And your fears—well, they're kind of outdated.

If you don't face your fears, you'll never know what you can actually do. We don't find our skills sitting on the couch watching TV. We find them when we put ourselves in uncomfortable and new situations. We realize that we're way more resourceful than we ever imagined. Because we have to be. Because we're pushed up against the wall, desperate, with no other options. That's when we learn what we're made of.

When you go back to face your fears, you realize that they really aren't fears anymore. You've grown and strengthened and changed into a new person. And fears are just the leftover remnants of who you used to be.

So clean off the cobwebs, take a look in the mirror, and thank the fear for trying to protect you. You don't need it anymore—you're on to bigger and better things. And that fear belongs in the past.

Nothing Can Ever Be as Scary as That

Conventional wisdom says that we should build up to our greatest fears. It encourages us to gain some strength, to do things when we're ready, to work toward our big goal. But this is our own path to success, remember? We're anything but conventional.

I've always valued life experience over other people's advice. And, when I was thirteen years old, I experienced the secret to overcoming any fear. See, I was terrified of rollercoasters. Completely terrified. I refused to go on any. Friends and family would bug me every time we were at an amusement park, but I was too afraid.

Now, my dad was strategic. He had a plan. He told me that he'd stop the incessant nagging if I'd go on just one rollercoaster of his choosing. Just one little rollercoaster, and then I'd never have to go on another in my entire life. I thought about the trade-off—two minutes of complete terror for a lifetime of freedom. It didn't seem so bad. He told me to close my eyes, and it'd be over in a few minutes.

Not knowing much about rollercoasters, I followed him into a line and sat down. I saw some other kids my age. It didn't seem so bad. Until we started to climb. And climb. And climb. I could see the parking lot from the top. I started screaming. I had no idea I was being manipulated like this. I agreed to *a little one*.

And then we dropped. I can still feel that drop in my stomach. It felt like it would never end.

When we got off, I stomped away angrily. I couldn't believe he had lied to me. But I couldn't wipe that secret smirk off my face. It really wasn't so bad. I survived. And no rollercoaster could ever be as scary as that one.

That's how I got over my fear of rollercoasters.

Like any skill, overcoming fear is a muscle that needs to be flexed. Fears don't just start overcoming themselves. You have to practice. You have to get up every day and do one thing that you're afraid of. One thing that you don't want to do at all. Even if it's small.

And, assuming you survive, you can move on to the next thing. And the next thing. And, all of a sudden, you're the guy or gal who can overcome fears. Because, for every fear that you overcome, you've got that in your back pocket. You know that nothing can be as scary as the thing that came before.

If you can survive that, you can survive anything. You can get on any rollercoaster you want. Because you're not afraid anymore.

The Stronger the Compass Points, the Closer You Are

But, when the fear's right in front of you, it's not so easy to just dismiss. We can call it whatever we want: resistance, procrastination, avoidance, self-sabotage, psychosomatic pain, hysteria. But the closer we get to success, the worse the fear seems to get.

The moments before we overcome another hurdle are always the scariest moments of the battle. We've gotten to the boss. We've reached our Bowser. Things are getting serious. This one's for all the marbles.

Any concerns of failure are going to be ten-fold. We start questioning if we're good enough or if we really deserve this. The moment of truth is upon us, and we want to turn around and march back to safety. The closer we get to success, the closer we get to an emotional breakdown.

We talk a lot of smack about emotional breakdowns, in whispered breaths and behind people's backs. We joke about it, we poke fun at it, we pity it. In reality, we're terrified of it ever happening to us. But we're looking at it all wrong. Emotional breakdowns have gotten a bad rap for long enough, and I'm here to settle the score.

As any good building contractor would know, you can't build that high-rise without stripping away the decrepit factory in its place first. Emotional breakdowns are about breaking down our old toxic emotional patterns so new ones can take their place.

Breakdowns aren't about being weak, they're about destroying all of those limiting beliefs that you weren't good enough, that you didn't deserve it, and that you're a total failure.

It's a lot easier to puff out your chest, crank up the defensiveness, and be "strong" than it is to push yourself through your own self-limitations and realize that the only thing holding you back is yourself.

We have so many layers of defense protecting us that we stop ourselves from doing anything unfamiliar. But the familiar hasn't worked out for us so far. It's time to push our limits and try something new.

When you feel the fear boiling up, when the resistance is overwhelming, when you want to turn around and run the other way, that's when you know something big is happening. You're right up against your walls. You're sure you can't go any further.

And then you blow through another limitation and keep charging forth toward success.

If you want to call it a breakdown, by all means, please do. But I prefer to call it a breakthrough.

Look for Your Own Reflection in Your Fears

Easier said than done, right? Sure, I can stand up here on my high horse (or behind the safe confines of book pages) and preach about overcoming your fears. But I have no idea what you're afraid of. I don't even really know what's going on in your life.

See, the interesting thing about fear is that it's totally subjective. It doesn't really matter what you're afraid of—that's pretty irrelevant. Anyone can be afraid of anything. And, for one person, the fear of failure could be just as paralyzing as snakes are to another. So fear says a lot more about you than it does about the person or thing you're afraid of.

It's about our own limiting beliefs. It's about the fact that we don't feel safe or qualified or good enough or able in the face of our fears. Because, when we're afraid, it means our mind is making an assessment that we're not safe if we move forward here. We've hit a boundary of what we think we can handle.

But, when we go right up to our fears—when we look the beast straight in the eye—we always see our own reflection. We always see ourselves, our beliefs, our limitations staring back at us.

Our culture's got it all wrong. We call anyone who can bungee jump, skydive, or wear booty shorts brave. But we're just projecting our own fears there. Bravery isn't about doing things that others are afraid of. It's about doing things that *you* are afraid of. It's about overcoming your own fears.

Slaying a dragon and standing up to your boss are both just inherently neutral actions. Neither is better than the other. It's what you had to overcome to get there that makes it heroic.

Don't get me wrong. You might fail. You'll probably fail—at least from time-to-time. But the greatest thing you can learn from your fears is that they're not outside of you. They're inside of you, and they've been there all along.

No one is ever going to give you permission to quit your job, ask for a raise, propose to your true love, climb that mountain, or write that book. If you want something, you have to give yourself permission to go after it. If you're afraid, then you've got to blow past those beliefs that you can't achieve it.

The thing that holds us back in this world isn't our abilities, it's our beliefs. Look the fear right in the eye and know that you are the one who created it. You can blow through it whenever you want.

When we move past our fears, we eliminate our boundaries. And a map without boundaries is limitless.

CHALLENGES

Complete the following challenges before moving on to the next chapter. To point yourself in the direction of success, you have to identify your biggest fears and the beliefs holding you back from overcoming them.

1. In your journal or on a private page that no one will see, make a list of the ten things you're most afraid of doing. Really put it all out there for this one. Everything from asking out that cute coworker to finally having that candid talk with your dad. Don't let rationalizations or excuses stop you from putting any fear down. Just think about the biggest blocks standing in the way of your success and jot them down.

2. Pick out the number one fear standing in your way of your new definition of success and decide to overcome it this week. Whether it's emailing your absolute hero, applying for your dream job, or dancing in the middle of the street, decide to just overcome it. Imagine what you could accomplish if you knew that you overcame this fear, regardless of the outcome. Then take a stand to stop thinking about it and just do it.

3. Get one of your biggest fears in your head—one of the really terrifying, blood-curdling fears that are standing in your way of success. Now close your eyes and let your mind drift back to when that fear started. Just see what pops up in your mind. It might not be what you

expected. It might have nothing to do with the fear. But notice where your mind goes and what you associate with that fear. Sometimes our fears are rooted in the most unexpected places. Open your eyes and decide to release the memory and the fear. The memory was in the past, and so is the fear.

4. Look at one of your biggest fears that's holding you back from success and think about what limiting belief you have attached to that fear. Are you afraid to give a speaking engagement because you feel like a fraud? Are you afraid to ask out that guy or gal because you don't think you're attractive? Trace your fears back to one particular limiting belief, and decide to work on changing that belief.

3

Your Poison Is Your Greatest Gift

"Don't be so sensitive."

I don't think there's a worse phrase in the English language. It's essentially telling you that you don't have a right to feel what you naturally feel. It's telling you that you're weak. That you're lesser. That your rational mind is overrun by emotions.

Ever since I was little, I was always on edge—anxious, stressed, nervous. I didn't like to be told I was wrong. I couldn't stand constructive criticism. And someone else's bad mood could ruin a night for me. So I did what any normal kid would do—I toughened up. I put on a thick defensive armor. Sensitivity was for weak people. And I wasn't going to be weak.

The second I was back to my normal health, the tough guy came right back out. *It wasn't a big deal. I didn't even need any medication. I figured it out. I could do it all alone. I was a tough guy.*

Only, this time, I couldn't hide my vulnerability. I started getting emails and Facebook messages from people I barely talked to who had heard about my sickness. They confessed to secret illnesses and embarrassments of their own. They wanted to know how I dealt with it all. They wanted me to share my experiences. They wanted to hear how I had to be seated next to the restroom in case of an emergency, or how I threw up in the middle of a restaurant. They didn't want the tough guy version—they wanted the raw stuff. They wanted to know that they weren't alone.

Maybe it was their all-too-familiar panicked tone. Or maybe it was the sheer number of requests I got. But something inside of me knew what I had to do. Emotional or not, I had to start writing.

Every day, as I shared another piece of my life, I was shocked by responses from friends and family, acquaintances and strangers, who related, empathized, laughed, or cried.

It seemed like the more I shared, the more I helped. The deeper I could go into my emotions, the deeper people appreciated. Tough guys and sensitives alike, they all encouraged my raw honesty.

It wasn't just about my sickness anymore. It was about me. A human being. Just another guy trying to figure it out. A guy who has fears and insecurities and doubts. Who is trying to create a successful life for himself.

I was sharing myself as vulnerably as I possibly could.

And then, one day, a reader wrote in, "I love your sensitivity. You seem to understand what people are going through and be able to talk to them in a very emotional way. You have a real gift."

And, whether I liked it or not, I had to agree.

What Weaknesses Are You Carrying Along?

We all know it. We've all been asked it before. That cliché interview question we cringe at: "What's your greatest weakness?"

We lie. We downplay. We turn our weaknesses into strengths. But, at all costs, we never expose anything truly vulnerable. That'd be detrimental. That'd be embarrassing. That'd be—well—weak.

As a society, we've learned to hide away any weaknesses. If we're naturally shy, we train ourselves to be outgoing. If we're sensitive, we learn how to be a tough guy. If we're slow or unskilled or handicapped at an activity in any way, we avoid it like the plague.

In our traditional success fairy tale, we know how to deal with strengths and weaknesses. We've got strengths, or skills that will help us propel forward to achieve lasting success. And we've got weaknesses, or potential roadblocks, which might stop us from reaching the gold.

In that story, success is easy. There's one strategy: maximize your strengths and minimize your weaknesses. Done. Easy. Piece of cake.

But my question is—who's judging which are strengths and which are weaknesses?

We're told from an early age that some of our traits are really useful, while others are completely useless. Right from the get-go, we're trained not to accept ourselves. We're taught that we have to downplay certain parts of ourselves because they're not totally helpful in society.

But that's only half the story. All growing up, I was quick-witted, perceptive, and discerning. I was also over-stressed, sensitive, and emotional. If those sound very similar, that's because they are. We're talking about an active nervous system in both situations. It's just viewed as a positive in some circumstances and as a negative in others. Characteristics by themselves are neutral; it's the context they're in that decides which are strengths and which are weaknesses.

Take the stubborn guy, for instance. On the one hand, he's impossible to negotiate with. He always has to get his own way, never willing to compromise. On the other hand, he sticks to his guns and refuses to let anyone push him around. Maybe as a salesman, he'd be viewed as pigheaded or difficult. But, as a small business owner, he'd be persistent and willful. Same trait, different context.

Or what about the focused lady? On the one hand, she can efficiently get all of her work done without paying attention to distractions. On the other hand, she can get so wrapped up in what she's doing that doesn't know when to quit. Maybe in the office, it'd be viewed as engaged and driven. At home, it might be obsessive and overly involved. Same trait, different context.

The point is that we don't have strengths or weaknesses. We just have a bunch of tools in the toolbox, which have varying degrees of success, depending on the situation. Sometimes it's better to be reserved, and other times out-going. Sometimes it's better to be goofy, and other times serious. We don't have strengths and weaknesses. We just have ourselves.

You Really Are a Product of Your Environment

I love Albert Einstein. There are few people who have street cred with the scientific community, the spiritual world, and serious and goofy folks alike. Naturally, I turn to him for a little sage wisdom on people's hidden strengths: "Everybody is a genius. But if you judge a fish by its ability to climb a tree, it will live its whole life believing that it is stupid."

Now, I'm no Einstein, but in my experience people who think they have limited talent tend to be the same ones barking up someone else's tree.

If the context you're in doesn't play to your strengths, pick another setting. This is your story, this is your life; you can write it any old way you want.

I'll give you an example. I know this graphic designer. For years, she was an office manager and a receptionist. She was easily bored, not so great with numbers, and spent a ton of time on social media. Needless to say, she wasn't producing her best work.

Ready for a change, she decided to quit and travel the world. She figured she'd find a way to make money on the road. In just a few short months, without any formal training, she became one of the most successful graphic designers in the country. She's able to constantly work on new projects, think of big-picture ideas on the fly, and advise on social media strategies. The talent was always there; she just needed a new context.

If you're a creative thinker who's waking up in the middle of the night to scribble down poetry, a typical nine to five might not be for you. If you're a couch potato who can't get anything started without a little kick in the pants, you might need more structure in your life. It's all about understanding your unique traits and how to give them the right environment to work for you. One's not better than the other; they just need different contexts.

Everything's Always Where You Least Expect It to Be

So how do you figure out what type of context you need to give yourself? Normally, most self-help gurus will tell you to focus on the skills that you already excel at. Those are your strengths. You usually want to structure your life around those.

Fortunately for you, I'm no guru. I'm just trying to help you carve out your own path to success. And, in case we haven't established it yet, I'm a little unorthodox.

I like to do things a little bit differently. So, with all due respect to colleagues and friends who've come before, I'm proposing a new way to find your strengths. I'm proposing you forget about everything you've ever been good at, at least for now.

Instead, think about what you really suck at. The stuff that you avoid at all costs. Your absolute worst weaknesses. The stuff that ruins your life. The embarrassing failures. The worst traits. Everything you wish you could change about yourself.

That's where your real strengths lie. If it can screw up your life that badly, imagine what it could do if you knew how to use it. All weaknesses are just strengths in hiding. It's your job to figure out how to lift that sword from its weakness-shamed stone.

So what are your worst weaknesses? I'm serious now. What are you worst weaknesses? Since we believe in the power of context now, just about anything can be a strength in the right environment.

The more it can screw up your life, the more powerful it must be—and the more likely it is to be one of your greatest untapped strengths.

The Alchemy of Turning a Weakness into a Strength

All of this everyone-gets-a-gold-star talk about how there are no weaknesses is nice. But let's get down to business here. How exactly do you turn your weaknesses into strengths?

Ironically, it's not what you have to do, but what you have to stop doing. We grow up learning what type of person we're supposed to be. We put the parts that align with that vision into a box called "strengths" and anything that doesn't into a box called "weaknesses." We split ourselves into good and bad, beautiful and ugly, perfect and flawed. We try to remove the parts we don't like, so we can head toward success.

The problem is that you're not just the "good parts." Whether you like it or not, this is a package deal. And, anywhere you go, the good, the bad, and the ugly is marching along with you.

No matter how rich or famous you get, the ugly parts will always be there. They could lash out and sabotage at any moment. They'll never go away. Because the ugly parts aren't just bad attributes, they're half of what makes up you.

To turn a weakness into a strength, you have to stop seeing the different categories. You have to empty those boxes. You have to stop trying to be who you're *supposed to be,* and start being who you already are.

You're a mixed bag. You've got strengths, weaknesses, skills, qualities, limitations, peculiarities—the whole bit. You're way too complex to be grouped into a couple of boxes. So don't let anyone try to force you to fit a stereotype—least of all yourself.

When we accept who we are, our whole selves, our complete selves, we learn how to tap into our inherent strengths. Because they're just a part of us.

Maybe you're the type who produces amazing work but needs two days of rest in between projects. Is that a strength or a weakness? Neither. It's just you.

Or maybe you're the type who can meet any last-minute deadline but can't get anything started unless there's someone breathing down your neck. Strength? Weakness? Let's just call it your own special brand of awesome.

In the right context, any traits can be absolute strengths. You've just been cast as the wrong role for far too long. It's time to change that. It's time to take the lead.

You Were Born to Thrive

But our culture values the *wrong* context. In fact, it's considered impressive to withstand horrible conditions. We love to brag about all that we can endure. Sleep-deprivation has become a badge of honor, stress is just par for the course, and back pain has almost become a cliché. We brag about everything from how much traffic we were stuck in to how long our days were. It's like we're expecting some reward for having the worst lives ever.

The truth is we're afraid. We're afraid to give ourselves what might really make us thrive. Because, if we did that, then we'd have no excuses left. And we're terrified that we still might fail anyway. There will be no one else to blame. No scapegoats to take the fall. Just us not being good enough. Confirming our worst fears.

So we endure. Just like the sore loser who gets a mysterious injury halfway through the game, we focus on the obstacles we've had to overcome rather than the results. Sure, the efforts seem impressive, but we never get to climb as high as we can. We'd rather take the easier route of staying stuck in the *wrong* context than risk gambling it all in the *right* one.

But, if you're serious about creating success on your own terms, then you're determined to blow through your own fears of success. You're not holding yourself back because you're afraid you won't make it. You're charging straight forward toward success. And you need to give yourself the context that fits.

You can endure in almost any context. We're made to endure. We adjust, tweak, compensate, maneuver to make it work. But there's a big difference between enduring and thriving.

Thriving is full of vitality, excitement, and passion. It's life—pure life just waiting to be unleashed. It's what turns tiny seeds into three-hundred-foot-tall trees. It's what changes struggling plants into luscious gardens. It's what transforms you from an average guy or gal into an overwhelming success.

We've all got different demands to make us thrive. We need different contexts. Some of us need to be surrounded by people, fueling us with energy. Others need constant quiet to crank out the next Great American Novel. Maybe a power nap would do you good. Or maybe you really do need ten hours of sleep. You could be an adventure-seeker hiking Mt. Everest. Or you could be a bookworm with your nose in your own type of adventure.

It's not about judging your needs. It's not about criticizing your ideal context. It's just about recognizing what it takes to make you thrive. It's about being honest with yourself and admitting that, in the right circumstances, any of us can be absolute geniuses.

It's about acknowledging that you've already got every tool you need to be successful. You just have to give yourself the right context for success.

CHALLENGES

Complete the following challenges before moving on to the next chapter. To build a successful life, you have to identify the circumstances that make you thrive and place yourself in the pathway of success.

1. Write down a list of your top ten weaknesses—the absolute worst things about yourself. The roadblocks and obstacles that always seem to get in your way. The things that screw up your life. The parts you wish you could change. Maybe it's the fact that you're needy in relationships, or the fact that you have to keep tweaking something until it's perfect. Jot those down.

2. Now look at the list of weaknesses you just made, and write next to each of the ten items just one instance in which somebody else with a similar trait is thriving. Maybe that person who's needy is a great parent because he's very attentive. Maybe that person who's a perfectionist is an amazing accountant because she always catches the error. Just write any ideas you have about some context in which that horrible weakness could look even remotely like a strength.

3. Think about how your current context is playing to your strengths or weaknesses. Are you a night owl who has to get up early for work? Are you a shy person who's thrown into boardroom presentations? Or maybe you actually have free time in the evening to meditate,

which allows you to decompress. Or you have a supportive relationship where you can vent your frustrations. Notice instances where your context is actually working against your natural inclinations, and where it's already working for you.

4. Give yourself permission to indulge your needs this week. Maybe you really need to cancel your after-work calendar and take a power nap every evening. Maybe you need to get a massage to de-stress from a crazy week. Do at least one thing that will make you thrive. And notice how your attitude and productivity are affected.

4

Let Passion Lead the Way

My entire career—entire life, really—I had given my voice away. I used my voice, my writing to make other people rich or famous or successful in some way. I was so focused on how I could use my skills for other people that I forgot what I actually cared about. My life was centered more around how I could impress people or make lots of money, and less around what I actually loved.

But there I was, blogging about myself. For the first time, I was sharing my sickness recovery story for anyone who was going through something and needed some support. I was sharing myself. Not a press release I'd penned or an op-ed I'd ghost written. Me. The real me. And the words just seemed to flow out of me. I didn't have to think twice about it. This voice just emerged . . . this voice I had never heard before. Or, at least, one I'd buried down long ago.

There was no real plan in mind. No real agenda to make money off of this. I just wrote because I loved it. I wrote because of the way it made me feel. I wrote because something happened during the process—something indescribable. And I knew that I just had to keep writing.

I was revitalized. I had more energy than I'd ever had. I looked forward to getting up and writing for people every day.

I had accidentally started seeing clients as a wellness coach. It wasn't my intention. But a friend of a friend needed help here and a relative over there. And, soon enough, I was open for business. Things seemed to be moving so rapidly that I didn't know how to stop them. It was like this just had a life of its own.

But there was the other thing: my day job. I was still working in public relations. And it was a great job—it really was. But, each day, I became less and less engaged in my work. I couldn't help but check who was commenting on my blog or emailing me for advice in between meetings. Whether I wanted to admit it or not, I had changed. A lot. This wasn't the same young, ambitious perfectionist from only months before.

I had gained something new. I had found my passion.

Pursuing it didn't make much sense. I was making money. Real money. Good money. Quite a bit of money. Why would I ever leave that? I liked what I did. I liked it a lot, in fact. But the truth remained, the truth I didn't want to admit: I didn't love it. I wasn't passionate.

Taking a leap from ensured success to almost definite failure seemed laughably foolish. There would be no safety net below. No get-out-of-jail-free card. No assurance that I'd land on my feet.

I was at the top of the cliff—a cliff that had taken me years to climb. And I watched my passion flying freely and perilously below.

Was "following your passion" just something that happened in the movies? Could things just magically work out?

It didn't make sense to anyone. Least of all me. But I closed my eyes and jumped.

How Do You Find Yourself?

A lot of people want to know how to find themselves. In fact, it's one of the most common questions I get.

I've always thought it was a funny question. I mean, there I am, looking right at the person. They look pretty found to me. So I've always given the best advice I could think of on the spot: "If you want to find yourself, you have to lose yourself first."

Losing ourselves isn't easy. We're always there. Always in our heads. Always thinking. We plan and strategize and analyze everything. We have backup plans and contingency plans. We like to feel in control. So we never let go. We never allow ourselves to be completely lost.

But even the most meticulous mind in the world can't plan every step of the journey. Inevitably, we're going to have to make some on-the-spot decisions. We're going to have to pick a road at the fork. And our logic can only bring us so far. If we could all rationalize our way to happiness, we'd all be there by now.

We need a light for those situations. A fire to illuminate the way. An internal flame that we can never lose for those dark and confusing moments. We need a passion.

On any good journey, a hero is faced with some kind of crossroads in a dark forest. That's just how cliché stories go. So it's wise to bring along a flame, to clearly show the potential paths we can take.

But most of us have no idea how to ignite our own fires, or passions, for that matter. See, when people ask me how to find themselves, what they're really asking me is how to find their passions. And that's easy. Passions are just the things that you lose yourself in. The things that take you out of your mind and into the world. The things that transcend time and energy. The things you could do all day (or night) with an infinite supply of vitality.

I don't need to tell you what lights your fire. You're already well aware. You wouldn't have made it this far in life if something didn't give you that rush. These days, life is too hard to live without it.

What are the things you could stay up all night talking about? What are the things you think about when you're daydreaming or listening to music? What are the things that you seem to have an endless supply of energy to do?

What makes you light up? What makes you raise your voice and flail your arms madly? What do you secretly research when no one's watching? What makes you forget about your worries?

Those are the things that make you lose yourself. They're the things that make you forget to be stressed or anxious. They're the things that make you drop all of your insecurities and fears. They make you forget how hard success is supposed to be because everything seems like so much fun.

When you lose yourself, you've just found yourself. Those are your passions.

But What if You're Not Passionate?

Okay, okay. I can talk a good game. But I know what you're thinking: you're just not that passionate. Nothing lights up your Christmas tree. You've seen those people who want to save the world, change healthcare, and build schools in third-world countries. You wish you had it, but that's just not you. You're more of a work, TV, sleep kind of guy or gal. You're cool with it. You've come to terms. You're just not that passionate.

I'm not even going to give you the proverbial smack across the face on that one. Just keep reading. If you don't have a passion, it's because you haven't let yourself.

When I was younger, my favorite movie was *Cinderella*. Yep, yep. Let's have a good laugh about it. But something about her impossible dream really stuck with me. I mean, here was a girl who didn't have a shot in hell at becoming a princess, and yet she still held on to this dream. The dream was so impossible, so preposterous, that most of us would have shut it down long ago. But she didn't.

From an early age, we're taught what is and isn't possible. We're short, so we're probably not making it in the NBA. We're chubby, so Olympic runner isn't in the cards. And, sooner or later, we settle on a small list of acceptable plans for our future. Maybe it's not everything we've ever dreamed of. Maybe it's not what we'd call an "impossible dream." But it suits us.

Except passion has almost nothing to do with skills. In fact, passion really has little to do with plausibility, either. It doesn't know what's possible or not; it just knows what gets your engine revved up.

If you think of anything that's ever excited you—from pretending you're Jack Bauer to playing cornhole at your college reunion—you're starting to tap in to your passions.

Passions don't have to be world-changing ideas. In fact, they hardly ever start out that way. They usually just start with a personal interest that might benefit someone else. And, when we combine multiple interests, we get one big passion.

Take the cornhole example. You like playing simple yard games with friends. You also used to enjoy coaching soccer and babysitting your cousin too. Could your passion be engaging children through games? Could you find a job as a camp director or fitness coach, or volunteer with a nonprofit? Could you start your own nonprofit using cheap yard games to create a community for inner-city kids?

I already feel the passion, and it isn't even my dream.

The point is that all of us have passions. Lots and lots of passions. We're just sucked into this thinking of what's possible and what's already been done before. But you're way better than that. Get creative. Think outside the box. Mix and match your interests. Consider how the world could be a better place. Pick up a hobby, some volunteering, a part-time job—anything that puts you in line with your passion.

There are many ways to infuse passion into your life. It's not that you're not passionate; you're just not being creative enough.

If there were no rules or bills or obligations, how would you spend your time?

The Burnout Myth

But, even if you were able to discover your passion, isn't there a chance that you'd just work on it until you burnout? We've seen countless examples of exhausted programmers, overworked executives, and frazzled artists. All great myths have a cautionary tale associated with them. In the case of the success story, it's burnout.

Burnout is the topic du jour. Companies and entrepreneurs across the country are warning about its allure. It's the temptation trap today's corporate climbers most easily fall into. We all know the formula. Married to work + sleepless nights + poor diet and exercise = burnout. Right?

Or not so much.

While I whole-heartedly agree that burning the midnight oil with an open bag of stale Doritos isn't exactly the path to sustainable success, burnout is about much more than work-life balance.

At the heart of it, burnout is really about your inner fire going out.

I know plenty of people who work nine to five jobs, sleep their solid eight hours, suck down their green smoothies, and make time for their families. And, guess what? A lot of them are burnt out too.

If you deprive a fire of oxygen, it'll suffocate immediately. If you don't feed your passion, you'll be suffocating that too. And no amount of sleep can rectify a loss of passion.

Of course, you can kill your fire by staying up all hours of the night working your butt off. But you can kill it just as easily by sitting at a desk when your heart is in front of a canvas. I know plenty of artists who've given up a night of sleep to work on a passionate project. They survived. I've never known a bored office worker whose extra sleep gave him more enthusiasm at work, though.

We have to stop pretending that we only gain energy through food and sleep. Anyone who's ever been jolted from the long day blues by surprise concert tickets, or perked up to play a game of soccer, knows exactly what I'm talking about.

Passion can fuel your energy tank when it's empty. It can make you sparkle when you're dull. It can reinvigorate you when you have nothing left to go on.

We're inspired by stories of the J.K. Rowlings and Oprah Winfreys of the world—people who started out with little more than passion to keep them going. Maybe they didn't have the ideal organic meal or perfect sleep routine, but passion sure gave them enough energy to get pretty far.

Don't mistake me though, folks. We'll even get sick of our favorite sushi roll if that's all we ever order. We're kidding ourselves if we think that a one-track mind is going to avoid burnout. Then we're no better than the miserable corporate drone who's trying to replace passion with a solid sleep cycle.

We're full of passions. Lots of passions. And the trick to never getting burnt out is to fuel each and every one of these passions. Maybe you're in the mood for a bad romantic comedy. Or it might be a good novel that feeds your soul. Of course, writing poetry could do the trick. Or better yet, it's working on a new start-up.

We've already established it: we're complex beings. We've got a whole bunch of passions. Sure, some things may really light our fires. But there are plenty more that need to be tended to on a cold winter night.

If we just focus on one passion all day, every day, we're inevitably going to burn out. We're going to use it up until it's dead. We need spontaneity. We need excitement. We need diversity to shake things up.

After a long day of work, take a long walk in the park. Or sit down and read some poetry. Or maybe even hit the yoga mat. Fuel each and every passion in your being.

The key to avoiding burnout is just doing what you love as much as possible. Pursue every passion, no matter how impractical or ridiculous it may be. Incorporate a variety of different passions into your day. Be honest with yourself, check in with your passions, and then feel free to indulge.

Because, if you restructure your life around what sets your heart on fire, that flame can never burn out.

Passion Is the Shortcut to Success

I grew up with Italians on one side of the family and Jews on the other. It wasn't exactly a quiet household. Voices were raised, feet were stomped, dishes were thrown. I know a thing or two about passion.

The thing about passion is you can't control it. You're in the middle of an argument, and the next thing you know, you're yelling and waving your hands around wildly. You just can't help yourself. It supersedes all logic. It throws all fears and insecurities to the wind. It's palpable. You can feel it in the air. You get so caught up in this frenzy that you often don't even remember what you were trying to accomplish in the first place—just that you're passionate.

Yeah, it's kind of like that. When we're pursuing our passions, we often forget that we're supposed to be insecure or afraid. We forget that work is supposed to feel like work. We even forget that we're desperately striving toward success.

Because we're not striving anymore; we're enjoying it. We forget to focus on the next step and moving forward because we're having a blast right where we are.

And people take note. Clients, customers, partners, investors—the whole shebang—want to get involved with whatever you're doing. Passion is contagious. People want to be a part of it. They want to be as happy and vibrant and full of life as you are. They want to work with you, learn from you, be a part of your vision.

When we approach our work from a place of passion, instead of a place of struggle, even the most disagreeable folks can't help but be persuaded. More business always starts to flock in. But, more importantly, so does more connection. Your passion resonates deep within your customers, and reminds them what they're passionate about. It's not just business anymore; it's inspiration.

Passion is really about turning work into play. And what adult doesn't need a little more play in his or her life?

Following your passion is the fastest way to hightail toward success. It trumps fears and worries. It brings customers to your front door. And it turns work into so much fun that you don't want to stop playing any time soon.

If that's not success, I don't know what is.

CHALLENGES

Complete the following challenges before moving on to the next chapter. To find your own path to success, you need to know what lights your fire and guides you in the direction of your dreams. A successful life is always beaming with excitement, vitality, and an overwhelming passion.

1. Write a fairy tale for yourself. Anything is possible. You can spend your days doing anything you want. You can have magical powers. The only restraints are the limits of your imagination.

   I. What do you do with your life? How do you spend your time? What do you contribute to the world?

   II. Remember that this is your ultimate fantasy, so it should be over-the-top fantastical. If you can't dream big in your fantasies, you won't be able to come close to that in real life.

   III. Now look at your story. How can you incorporate just one of those dreams into your real life today? Make a plan to implement one aspect of your dream life today.

2. Without thinking, make a list of everything that you love doing. Write down everything that you could stay up all night talking about, that you daydream about, that you get energized just thinking about. Maybe you're into playing cards or arguing about politics.

Maybe you're more of a sports fanatic or a fitness fiend. Just throw it all down on paper and get to know what your passions are. Your decisions toward success will be guided by if they're bringing you closer to or further from these passions.

3. Make a list of the top five passions that refuel you. They can be anything from watching an episode of *Mad Men* to going for a run. The only rule is that you have to love doing it, and it has to always nourish and refuel your system. This is now your Burnout Avoidance Cheat Sheet. Put this list somewhere where you will see it throughout your day—in your bedroom, on your computer, stuck on your fridge. Whenever you are feeling exhausted, stressed, or totally burnt out, do at least one thing from the list to refuel yourself. Giving some love to all of your passions is the key to overcoming burnout.

5

A Quitter Calls it Failing, a Hero Calls it Learning

Fast forward a year. After finding a replacement at my job and finishing up nutrition school and herbalism school, I was ready to embark on my own adventure.

I had left my job in public relations. I was on my own. The world was my oyster. In my mind I imagined days spent changing people's lives. In my heart I felt accomplished, free, and powerful. But in my ears I heard . . . crickets.

I had put my blood, sweat, and tears into growing my business as fast as possible, and the only thing that was coming in was bank statements to let me know that my savings were quickly dwindling.

I gave talks that were total busts. I wrote articles that few people paid attention to. I went to networking parties and industry events all across the city. And I just ended up with one disappointment after another.

Failure. Failure. Failure.

I sat in my empty office, wondering if maybe I wasn't really cut out for this. Maybe I was just kidding myself.

Maybe the secure job with good money was the absolute right choice.

I said I wanted to do what I loved, not what made me money. I said I was better than that. And, there I was, at the end of my rope, willing to take in anything that would pay me.

The lavish freedom, the complete control—all of it was a myth. I was typing articles, scheduling meetings, and planning talks day-in and day-out. I spent more time with my computer than I ever had in public relations. I wasn't this glamorous entrepreneur. I was a broke dude trying desperately to appear successful.

Worst of all, I was supposed to be coaching people on how to build successful companies without getting burnt out. I was supposed to help people define success on their own terms. And the only two things I felt were burnt out and unsuccessful.

I was a total failure. I was ready to pack up, throw in the towel, and go home.

Before I decided to pack it all in, I took one last look at my website. There was a picture of me in a suit with some professional language. It didn't feel like me at all. It felt like some other guy trying to be something he just wasn't. It felt like me trying to achieve someone else's version of success that I never wanted in the first place.

I immediately called a web designer and got to work. If I was going to do this, I was going to do it on my terms. Failure felt more like a wake-up call than anything else.

And I wasn't about to give up.

The End of Failure

Whenever somebody mentions success, there's always that automatic association with failure. We know it well. Fear of failure is the number one obstacle to success. We're so terrified of doing anything because *we might fail*. We don't want to take chances because they might not work out in our favor. That start-up could go under. That presentation could be a bust. That prospective customer could laugh in our face. That new blog might not get any readers. There are so many ways to fail that it's almost paralyzing to even mention the word.

There's such a finality to failure. It's failed. Done. Over. Zip. There's no real coming back from there. If you failed, you failed. Whatever you were doing has ended, and you can't go back.

Honestly, the way people talk about failure, I'd think they were talking about death. We're terrified of it, it's in the back of our minds at all times, and we're sure that there's no coming back after we've failed. Failure is the end. Once you fail, whatever you were doing is over, and you have to give up.

But take it from a guy who fails on a pretty regular basis: the world doesn't really end. I trip all the time. Did I fail at walking? *Yep.* Do I get back up? *Usually with a self-conscious scan to see who was watching.*

I mispronounce words. I stutter during talks. I make typos. I send in bad articles. I forget birthdays. I get lost while driving. I fail all the time. And I'm pretty sure I'm still kicking.

Failing doesn't make me a failure. It makes me human. It gives me a lesson. It teaches me how to fix things. I'll never make the same mistake twice. And, when I do, then I'll learn not to make cheesy blanket statements.

We never stop learning. Even if we try, we can't stop learning. We're always going to make mistakes. We're always going to do things wrong. The fun in being imperfect is that there's always more to learn. We're doing the best we can right now, and when we "fail," we'll learn a better way to do it.

Failure is an important part of the success journey because it's the only way that we grow. Without failure, we'd just keep doing the same thing over and over. *Why fix what isn't broken?* But failure gives us the opportunity to experiment, try new things, learn from our mistakes. Maybe that way didn't give us the result that we were looking for, but this way might be more effective. It's not failure, it's trial-and-error. That's the only way we really learn things. We learn from our experiences. We learn from our successes. But, most of all, we learn from our failures.

So who's judging what's a failure and what's a lesson? You are. You're the only person who can decide that you've failed. If it wasn't a failure, then it's just a lesson. It's just an opportunity for you to learn more about how to be successful. Any time that you've decided that you've failed, know that it was your decision. No one else could decide it for you. No one else determined that you had to stop tweaking the model or trying new techniques.

Failure is only failure if we decide it is. By all means, you can quit at any time. But, if you've still got another round in you, then let's take the lesson and keep jabbing. We're not done yet, and there's still work to do while we're here.

You Already Learned Everything about Failure in Preschool

Let's start with the basics. As much as I can try to tell you about failure, you've already learned everything you need to know about it when you were five years old. You were playing with building blocks. Sometimes the blocks didn't fit together in the right way. Sometimes the entire structure would even collapse. But you just kept on building and playing. It was fun, even when it didn't work out. And you eventually learned the best way to put them together and build a solid structure.

When you got bored, when you were ready to quit, you stopped. Nobody forced you to quit. Nobody said that you messed up too many times and it was over for you. You just played until you were done playing. You did things on your own terms.

When we get older, we forget that we're just playing. We start taking everything so seriously. We forget that we're just learning how to fit the blocks together in the best way. We can't expect to know how to do it from the get-go; we've never done this before.

When we're older, we get mad every time we make a mistake. We freak out when the structure collapses. We think there's no way in hell that we can rebuild the entire thing. Over is over. We forget about all those times that we just put the pieces back together until we built something again. And how much fun we had doing it.

We need to remember that we're just playing. That life is about playing around. It's about trying to fit the pieces together. Sometimes it works, sometimes it doesn't. But we can keep playing and learning until we're ready for something new.

Who vs. What

So why do we get so upset when something goes wrong? Why are we so attached to every little outcome? Why do we view it as a failure and not as a lesson?

Think about what happens when you first meet people. If your experience is anything like mine, the same thing happens every time. Rain or shine, rich or poor, small town or big city, I'm always asked the exact same question upon meeting someone: "What do you do?"

Now, I'm not excusing myself here. I'm just as guilty as the next guy (or gal). I follow (most) social norms just like the rest of you, and I've asked it from time-to-time.

And it makes sense. Most of us spend over half of our waking hours working every weekday. That's a whole lot of time spent at work. We can talk about the weather, we can talk about politics, but our bread and butter is really how we spend most of our days.

But what if that went away tomorrow? What if we lost our jobs? Got demoted? Got up the nerve to quit? How would we introduce ourselves? How would we start conversations?

Who would we be without the *what?*

We've come to over-identify with our jobs so much that we internalize them as a part of *who* we are. We judge personalities based on job stereotypes (e.g. accountants are boring, lawyers are sharks, and artists are flaky). We make relationship decisions based on what job our partner has. And we determine our own self-worth according to how we make our money.

Without our jobs, we wouldn't be ourselves. Now, no wonder failure feels a little bit like death. It kind of is. If we *fail* at our careers, it's like a part of us dies.

We want to be happy, successful, fulfilled. But the only way we know how to get there is to do good work, make lots of money, and act important. We try to *do* our way into *being* all the time. No surprise that we confuse the two.

But leaving your job doesn't really change who you are. Totally flopping on sales doesn't really, either. They're just things you do. Actions. Sometimes they work, and you keep with that strategy. Sometimes they don't, and you modify and make a new one.

But actions are never essence. They can never really change your passions or abilities or talents. They can't really touch anything inherent in you. They're just stuff you do that gets particular results. If you don't like the results, change the actions. But don't ever change yourself.

What you are isn't *who* you are. And *who* you are is a whole lot more interesting.

Public vs. Private

But would you care a whole lot less about your failures if they were private? I mean, do you shame yourself when you're cooking alone and you burn the mushrooms? Do you beat yourself up for making a typo in your journal entry?

In other words, in the proverbial forest of life, if you failed when nobody else was watching, would the failure still make a sound? Are you more afraid of failure or of what people will think of that failure?

If we're being honest, we care what people think. *Yes, even you.* We all want to be well-liked, respected, impressive. Hell, isn't that half the reason we want to be successful in the first place? So, failing sucks. But failing publicly is on a whole other level.

The truth is that looking stupid is more mortifying to us than failing at all. When somebody judges our failure, it's a lot harder to see it as a lesson. We just look silly, and that's really embarrassing for us, whether we're trying to learn from it or not.

But the path to success is lined with embarrassing mistakes. To create any real version of success, you're going to look stupid. A lot. You're going to do things for the first time. Things you've never done before. You're going to publicly embarrass yourself. You're going to have to admit that you're not perfect, that mistakes happen, and that you'll do your best to recover. But public humiliation is pretty much inevitable.

The first time I used chopsticks in public, I looked ridiculous. But I couldn't expect myself to magically know how to use chopsticks without ever trying. The first time I wrote an article, it really sucked. It took time for me to refine my skills.

There are very few instances where any of our first attempts are going to be good. But that doesn't mean we should stop ourselves from doing them. It doesn't mean we should judge ourselves for looking foolish. If anything, we should proudly show the world that we're trying something new and are unafraid to suck at it. That isn't embarrassing—that's sexy. We're confident enough to look bad, or at least we're faking the confidence to do so.

Let yourself look stupid. Let yourself flop in public. Realize that it's not over. You'll survive. And you'll go on to get really good at whatever you sucked at. But, if you aren't willing to mess up royally in front of a whole crowd, you'll never be successful in front of one either. To be a public star, you have to risk being a public failure first.

The Fail-Proof Formula

You're probably reading this and nodding your head in agreement. Maybe you'll even jot a little line on a Post-it and stick it to your desk.

But, inevitably, failure is going to come upon you, and you're going to freak out like there's no tomorrow. In those situations, no advice in the world will be a squat of help. So, instead of being overrun by the failure frenzy, let's just step around it. Let's just decide to avoid failure altogether.

After years of failing—and failing hard, I might add—I've come up with a formula to avoid the process completely. To just step around it, like some dog poop in the street.

Replace the world "failed" with "adapting."

Simple, right? Too simple. There's no way that could work.

Okay, let's try it:

"My business model failed because customers didn't want to buy at my price."

BECOMES

"My business model is adapting to better meet the needs of my customers."

Okay, this is fun. Let's do another one:

"I failed at winning the investors over with my presentation."

BECOMES

"I'm adapting my presentation deck to be more accessible to investors."

All right, one more. Now I'm just getting cocky:

"I failed at asking that cute girl out last night."

BECOMES

"I'm adapting my approach to dating because I haven't found the right fit."

You don't have to worry about turning failures into lessons, because there's no real failure in sight. In adapting, you're taking the lesson a step forward and running with it. You're implementing it directly into your life.

So your company isn't doing as well as you wanted it to. You adapt and pick up a part-time job while you work on it. Is that failing? Not really.

So you get passed over for that promotion. You adapt and decide to finally start looking for a new job. Have you totally failed? Don't think so.

The point is that nothing is ever over until it's over. If you have the passion and drive, you can keep adapting every which way. You can pick up part-time jobs, and volunteer, and make connections, and tweak the business model, and do whatever else you need to do to keep your dream alive.

It's failure when you're ready to throw in the towel and be a quitter. There's nothing wrong with that. You're welcome to quit at any time. You just have to acknowledge that it was a conscious decision to quit. That you never really failed.

And, if you're not ready to hang yourself out to dry just yet, you're just adapting. You're just tweaking. You're just playing around, trying to figure out the best way to make your dreams come true.

Remember, this is your life. This is your game. You can't fail if you make up the rules.

CHALLENGES

Complete the following challenges before moving on to the next chapter. There will always be obstacles, setbacks, and missteps on the road to success. It's up to you to decide if they're failures that stop you dead in your tracks, or lessons to help you propel forward.

1. Make a list of ten things you've failed at in life. It can be anything from ending a relationship, to losing a job, to botching a science class experiment. Next to each, write down one lesson that you learned from these failures. You might have learned what you really wanted in a relationship, how to be more assertive, that you needed to improve your people skills, that science just wasn't for you. Circle any of them in which you felt like the failure was worth it. Now try to remember this exercise every time you feel like you've failed at something new.

2. Consider your biggest failure so far in life. Think about why it was such an important failure. Why did it mean so much to you? Why were you so attached to these particular actions? Notice in what area of life the failure occurred. Was it in your relationship, your work, your family life, maybe even sports? Understanding where you hold the most shame from your "failures" will give you a clue into where you most strongly attach *who* you are to *what* you do.

3. Try something new this week. Something that you're afraid of trying. Something that you'll probably suck at. Put yourself out there and make yourself try something way out of your comfort zone. Maybe it's acting class or painting. Maybe it's a game of volleyball or ballroom dancing. Whatever you choose, allow yourself to risk failing. If you fail and you survive, you realize it wasn't so bad. You can always pick it up again and keep doing it until you succeed.

4. Think about the number one thing you are failing at right now on your success journey. Are you not picking up enough clients? Are you not finding the love of your life? Are you not making money? Just choose the number one failure and write it down on a piece of paper.

  I. Now use the Fail-Proof Formula and turn that failure into an adaptation. What are you adapting right now? Are you adapting your marketing strategy to attract more clients? Are you adapting your approach to dating?

  II. Finally, actually get out there and start adapting exactly what you said you would. Try new things. Dare to fail again. And dare to adapt another time.

6

This Might Be Your Adventure, but It's Not All about You

I spent the next few months really infusing myself into the business. I was more honest in my branding. I let my personality shine through. I decided to work with the clients that I wanted, not just anyone and everyone.

I felt like I was really learning the lessons of my failures. I adapted, and I was really happy with the result.

But I still wasn't attracting clients. And the ones I had weren't achieving the type of success that I was promising. My talks all felt awkward and uncomfortable. My workshops were even worse.

I was flopping left and right. No matter what I did, I struggled. I tried everything from business training to having a personal coach. None of it seemed to matter. I wasn't enough.

I was determined to be a better coach. To give better advice. To say the right thing. To change my clients' lives.

As I furiously wrote in my journal about my experience, I started to count the number of I's on the page. There was no mention of clients. No thought about what they were thinking or feeling. No real concern about why they weren't hiring me or engaging or succeeding. I was making my business of service all about me.

So I took a backseat. I stopped trying to prove myself so much. I stopped talking, period. I just let the clients voice their concerns. I let them lead the discussions. I started getting inside their heads, thinking like them, figuring out what their root problems really were.

And, like magic, things started improving. People were having success story after success story. And—quite frankly—I was hardly doing anything. I wasn't teaching people what to do. All I was doing was getting out of the way.

I found that people will tell you exactly what's wrong and exactly what they're looking for, if you listen closely enough. The problem was, I was so obsessed with how I was performing that I didn't want to listen to my clients.

It may have been my party, but it definitely wasn't all about me.

No One's Watching That Closely

Have you ever given a speech in front of a large crowd? If you're anything like me, your palms get sweaty, your knees buckle, and your voice quivers a little bit. You might stumble over a few words or start speaking way too fast. And, once you start noticing how you're doing, forget about it. The rest is just downhill. So you slink off the stage, hoping the memory of your talk is soon forgotten.

But the crowd applauds in awe. They didn't notice the sweaty palms or the buckling knees. They paid no attention to the quivering, stumbling, fast-paced voice. In fact, they thought you nailed it.

And you're thinking to yourself, *Were they even watching the same talk?*

Yeah, life is kind of like that. We can probably drop the insecurity because no one is paying nearly as much attention to us as we think they are. They're too busy in their own heads worrying about their own insecurities.

We're a self-centered bunch, you know that? We have this amazing ability to somehow make everything about us. We attend a funeral and worry that the flowers we bought were too showy. We bring food to a potluck and obsess over how much people have eaten our pasta salad compared to the neighbor's. In almost any situation, we can turn ourselves into the center of attention when, in fact, it has nothing to do with us.

I'm going to bet that your definition of success involves helping people in some way. Apart from spending the rest of your life meditating in solitude, there's no definition of success that is independent of people. No matter what, you're always in service of someone else. So it's not really about you.

If you've got a boss, you're working for him. If you've got clients or customers, you're answering to somebody. And, if you care about anybody at all, even a little bit—well, you get the point.

We give talks to educate, inspire, or entertain others. We build products to make people's lives just a tad bit better. We create services to revolutionize the way certain things are done. Hell, we even tell jokes just to make people smile.

So, if our real aim is to create our version of success by improving the lives of others, then why are we so wrapped up in ourselves?

Get Out of Your Own Way

A few years ago, my brother-in-law Mike, an EMT at the time, was enjoying a lazy Saturday off work and on the couch, when something from his dispatcher caught his attention. An emergency was being reported at his parents' address. Without even thinking, he jumped in his car and drove straight to the scene. Mike found his father lying unconscious, blue in the face, without a pulse. He had had a heart attack. Instinctively, Mike grabbed the defibrillator and immediately starting zapping his dad. The ambulance arrived moments later. To the paramedics' shock, the previously pulse-less man was back to breathing. If Mike hadn't arrived when he did, his father would have been dead. Mike saved his life.

When asked what he was thinking during the situation, Mike admitted that he wasn't thinking. He didn't question if he could actually do this. He didn't think about the emotional connection. He didn't worry that he hadn't showered, or about how he parked, or about what people thought. He just did what he had to do. He trusted himself because he had no other choice.

I love this story. Not just because it's an account of unbelievable heroism and miracles, but because it reminds me of what can happen when you get out of your own way.

Somewhere deep inside, we all have the most unbelievable abilities. Maybe we aren't all EMTs, but there's some intelligence in there just waiting to come out. If you can just trust yourself to take charge, you probably have the right answer in there. But, unfortunately, it usually isn't until emergency situations that we throw away all of our frantic insecurities and excuses, and let it shine through.

We're so worried that we'll say or do the wrong thing. We worry about how we'll look. We stress about what people will think. We're convinced that we don't know enough. Because we don't trust ourselves. We don't think that we can actually do it. We don't feel good enough. So we get in our own way.

When we don't trust ourselves, we close up. We hold ourselves back from offering what we know. Because we don't think it will be enough. We don't think we can really help. We don't think we have enough experience or knowledge or wisdom. So we overanalyze every step of the process, instead of just trusting what naturally comes out.

It's like giving a speech. The more you focus on your awkward hand gestures or the sound of your voice, the more likely you are to lose your train of thought or stumble over words. But, when you get so passionate about what you're saying that you forget to be nervous, you're an all-star. You say things you didn't even realize you knew. You put together new ideas on the spot. You're able to trust that you have everything you need inside of you; you just have to give it an opportunity to come out.

The number one skill you can cultivate for success is self-trust. A tiny seed has all the intelligence it will ever need to be a three-hundred-foot tree. You have in you all the intelligence you will ever need to be undeniably successful. You can add in more knowledge any time you want. You can keep gaining new experience. But you are good enough right now. You have enough intelligence in you right now. You just have to learn how to trust yourself.

And it's a lot easier to choose to trust yourself now than to wait for an emergency situation to put you in the hot seat.

Get Comfortable Being Naked

The main reason that we can't get out of our own heads and trust ourselves is that we feel like frauds. We don't feel good enough or smart enough or qualified enough. So we throw on a suit and tie and act professional. Or we write ourselves a script before the meeting. Or we pretend we know exactly what our client is talking about as we're secretly Googling from the other end of the phone call. But under no circumstances do we let our walls down. Under no circumstances do we drop the mask. Under no circumstances do we get vulnerable.

We want to be polished, professional, put together, and everything else business school tells you to be. So we edit that blog post five hundred times before it goes out. We rehearse that speech until we're saying it in our sleep. And we refuse to launch our new website until it's damn near perfect.

But, whether you want to believe it or not, a wardrobe malfunction is bound to happen sooner or later. You're not going to catch that glaring typo, or you're going to completely lose your train of thought in the middle of a speech. And you'll be totally exposed as the fallible, mistake-ridden, vulnerable human that you are. So you might as well get comfortable being naked.

The more layers we put on to hide ourselves, the further away our customers, clients, even potential lovers are from getting to know the real us. But creating success on your own terms has to be natural. It has to be honest. It has to feel like you.

Nobody wants the generic professional guy, anyway. The one who wears the right suits. The one who says the right things. He's polished, he's put together, and he's always looking for the next opportunity. Professional? You betcha. Likeable? Not even a little bit.

We're no cookie-cutter crowd. We like our businesses cooked a little raw. We like some authenticity infused in.

We love hearing from the health coach who's honest about still struggling with that extra weight. We love hearing from the stress expert about her own hectic household. We don't like perfect. We like real. It adds more credibility.

We cheer for the underdog. We love to watch a good rally. And we're inspired when people do it their own way, not the way everyone else does it.

Professionalism is great. It's perfect and put together and infallible. But here's the thing about professionalism: There's nothing passionate about it. There's nothing raw and visceral and magnetic about it. It's kind of . . . fluff. It doesn't get you inspired or angry or emotional in any way. It doesn't move people to do much of anything.

You don't really want to be professional, at least not deep down. Because you know that you're more inspired than that. You know that you're more interesting than that. You know that it might not be the most professional thing in the world, but pausing for a midday dance break brings life back into the office.

Every good salesman in the world knows that real business deals don't happen in an office. They happen at sporting events or over dinner. They happen on the golf course or while secretly bashing competitors. They happen in the most unprofessional of situations.

People like to remember that they're alive and that they're human. We have enough out there trying to convince us that we're just a bunch of robots.

So, add a little sass to your demeanor. Spice up your sales pitch with a little humor. Show us that you're unique, you're human, and you're unmistakable.

You don't need professionalism to rock it. You can just be you.

The Real Secret to Success

Okay, rock stars. Before you get carried away with your newfound spunkiness, let's remember that this isn't really about you to begin with.

If you want to be successful, there's one thing that will take you there faster than anything else in the world. One thing that will, hands down, trump all else every single time. And I'm willing to bet all my credibility on it. Improve people's lives. Significantly and consistently.

That's it. That's the real formula. If you figure that out, you can pack up and go home right now. You've got it. You've continuously made life after life better in a big way.

Success has almost nothing to do with you and everything to do with those you serve. I don't care if you are a gas station attendant or a nonprofit CEO. If you can make people's lives significantly better on a regular basis, you will be successful, no matter what your definition of that is.

Don't believe me? Here's an example: I knew a man who loved making sandwiches but had absolutely no money to open a shop. He rented out a small corner of a convenience store in a poor neighborhood and bought himself an electric griddle. He could only make one sandwich at a time, and it usually took a while. So he started talking to the customers—finding out about their lives, sharing wisdom he received throughout the years, creating a real connection in the few minutes he had. He'd crack jokes and give people nicknames. He'd let regulars invent their own sandwiches.

And, before he knew it, people started lining up to come to the shop. They would have to wait longer than any other shop in the city. They would deal with the tiny, smelly location. They even admitted that the sandwiches themselves were just okay. But they kept coming back, just to talk to the sandwich maker.

He knew how to improve people's lives significantly and consistently.

If you can give people what they really want, not just what they think they want, you'll be an instant success. If you can honestly improve lives every day, people will keep coming back.

The point is that it doesn't really matter how well you cook or perform or do business. It's not even about you in the first place. It matters how much your audience benefits from your work. It matters how well your work is received.

If you stop focusing on yourself and start giving people what they want, there's nothing you can't accomplish.

CHALLENGES

Complete the following challenges before moving on to the next chapter. To create success, you have to learn to get out of your own way and trust yourself, so you can make a difference in people's lives. Instead of focusing your attention on your own insecurities, turn your attention to the ways that you can help your audiences.

1. Remember a time when you thought you absolutely bombed on a project, only to be praised by everyone around you. Write down this memory and keep it in your pocket. Whenever you're feeling stressed, insecure, or troubled, pull out the memory and realize that it's not about you, it's about the benefit people get from what you do. If you give it your all, it's out of your hands. You have no control over how people will react.

2. Think about one of your particular audiences, whether it's clients, customers, a boss, a significant other, or a new friend. Instead of thinking what you can share with them, flip the thought and write down what this audience needs from you.

   I. Maybe you're a life coach and the audience needs clarity. Then it doesn't really matter how many brilliant things you say, it just matters that they clarify their thoughts. Or maybe you run a web-based marketplace that sells organic foods. Then it doesn't really matter how trendy your look is, it matters

more that the food is easy to purchase, and customers know where it's coming from.

    II. Make a list of at least ten wants and needs that your
audience has. When you flip the thought from what
you give to what they need, you set yourself up to
create success.

3. Write down any insecurities you have that you're trying
to cover up. Maybe you feel inexperienced to do the
type of work that you do. Maybe you feel that people
don't take you seriously enough because you're young.
Maybe you don't think you're good looking enough to
be on TV.

    I. Now push yourself to own that insecurity and turn
it into a point of differentiation. If you're inexperienced, maybe you bring a fresh perspective to the
industry. If you're young, maybe you can speak to
a whole new audience. If you're not a glam model,
maybe you can be an inspiration for everyday
people.

    II. The anxieties and insecurities that make you "less
professional" also differentiate you so that prospective clients and customers can distinguish you from
the generic norm.

4. Make a list of all the ways that you already improve
people's lives significantly and consistently. You might

be a good listener and give advice to all of your friends. You might always tell funny stories that bring people out of a bad mood. You might have a knack for getting people to dance and loosen up at weddings.

I. Infuse those abilities to improve people's lives straight into your business and life. Even if it doesn't necessarily match up with your business, find a way to give your gift to your audience. Those are the things you're going to be remembered for. People can hire any marketing consultant. But, if you're the marketing consultant who can do great work *and* make them laugh, you're the best guy or gal for the job.

7

Let Stress Be Your Mentor

The truth is I've never dealt with stress that well. No matter how much I was coaching people on stress management, I'd always turn into a raving lunatic in my personal life.

I got stressed easily. Anything could set me off. And, once the stress ball started rolling, there was just no stopping it.

At least in PR, I understood where the stress was coming from. I could pin it on deadlines, 24/7 news cycles, and catching every typo. That made sense to me. Surely, I wasn't the stresspot. I just had a stressful job.

But, once I left PR, the stress didn't just magically disappear. I was still jumping at client emails. I was still working late days. I still felt guilty any time I'd go for a midday walk or I'd get an afternoon massage.

I was stressed about everything from being responsible for client's successes to feeling irresponsible for taking time for myself.

If anything, my life got more stressful once I was on my own. Because all of the excuses had gone away. I had all the time in the world. I had earned more than enough to live off of. I had relatively few responsibilities. And yet I still felt trapped. I was still completely stressed.

The stress wasn't out there. It was in here.

It was easier to pin it on something else. The money issues. My lack of time. A million chores. Being exhausted. Annoying clients.

But, when I stripped all of that away, I still just saw myself staring back in the mirror. The guy who was completely stressed out. And I knew I had a problem.

If I was going to be successful, I was going to have to learn how to manage stress on my own. I was going to have to stop viewing it as an enemy and start seeing it as a teacher.

Because stress was the one thing holding me back from success—and there was no one left to blame.

It was time to make friends with stress.

The Word that Launched a Thousand Heart Attacks

Somewhere in every journey, an all-knowing, impossible-to-understand mentor comes along. *Star Wars* had Yoda. *Karate Kid* had Mr. Miyagi. We have stress.

Stress. Just seeing that word makes me tense up. We know the feeling. We've felt it many times before. The tense muscles, the racing heartbeat, the increased sweating. It's what keeps us up all night worrying about the next day's big presentation. It's what keeps us checking our email instead of relaxing on the beach. It lurks around every corner, hiding in bills and deadlines and relationship troubles.

Could this really be our mentor? We don't want to learn anything from stress—except maybe how to avoid it.

But what exactly *is* this thing that we're trying to avoid and manage? What exactly is it that we're all shaking in our boots over? What exactly is stress?

We've all got our own favorite variety of this faceless foe. My definition of stress is very different from yours. The things that stress me out are probably wildly different from the things that stress you out. Whereas I call it criticism, horror movies, and parallel parking, you might see stress as your mother-in-law stopping by on laundry day. So, if stress is unique to each of us, that means that we're part of the equation. We're co-conspirators in this heart-pumping heist. And stress is just pointing out our role in it all.

The truth is that stress is just our body's physiological response to a thought or emotion. We're the ones producing the thought. We're the ones letting our bodies know that we don't feel safe because we might miss our deadline. We're the ones telling our bodies to pump up the cortisol because it's going to be a long night.

Fifty thousand years ago, that same stress response was the only thing tightening our muscles, widening our eyes, and pumping enough oxygen into our system to fight or flight. We may have replaced tigers with mortgages and lions with performance reviews, but that age-old response is still teaching us when it's time to fight and when it's time to flight today. We've just forgotten how to listen to our mentor.

Time to Fight

Stress isn't all bad. Truth be told, it comes in handy some-times. The stress of a deadline is what's making me write this section right now instead of just watching TV. Stress about your big presentation gives you the energy to stay up late and finish it. Stress during an emergency is what sharpens an EMT's focus to make those split-second deci-sions. Stress provides us with motivation, energy, strength, and focus. In small doses, it's our most effective tool for charging forward. We couldn't even come close to success without it.

But that type of stress only works when it's time to fight. Productive stress is the kind of stress you can use to make something happen, like finish a project before the deadline, finally stand up to your boss, or give somebody emergency CPR. It's our battle cry. It's that urge to fight and create the lives we've always wanted. It pumps adrenaline and cortisol through our veins, it spikes our blood sugar, it gives us the tools we need to survive an acute fight. Without productive stress, we would never be moving toward our dreams.

When you're feeling the stress response come on, see if you can use it. Can you use that extra energy to finish the project? Can you think quicker in a meeting? Can you sprint down the street to catch the store before it closes? If you can do something with it, then it's productive stress. It's the kind of stress that improves your life because it moti-vates you to take action and fight.

Productive stress makes that beating heart and shortness of breath our ally. It's working for us. It's exactly what we need to teach us how to fight for what we want. We need that little spark of passion in our lives. That's what drives us toward success.

Ready for Flight

But what about when you can't use it? Productive stress is absolutely great for the few times that you can actually use it, but what about the other 99 percent of the time? Like when you're stuck in a sea of traffic, screaming like a madman? Or when you're sitting behind a computer feeling tense over that email from your boss?

That, my friends, is when it's time for flight.

Stress is constantly sending us messages. When we used to see predators in the wild, the message was crystal clear: stop doing what you're doing and run. But the message is a lot more confusing when you're just running late for dinner plans. There's no sharp-toothed creature about to maul you down for arriving late, so what gives?!

Remember that stress is just your body reacting to some thought or emotion—some perceived danger. If we're feeling the stress come on and we can't use it to our advantage (i.e. it's not productive), then it's pointing out that something's amiss, and it's time to send it to flight. Maybe there's a destructive thought, belief, or behavior that needs to go. Maybe there's a bad gut feeling telling us that business proposal is bad news. Unproductive stress always warns us about some attitude or action that's holding us back from success.

Honking your horn while stuck in traffic might mean that you need to stop overbooking yourself and cushion in extra time for things like traffic. Tightened stomach before a meeting could be a limiting belief that you're not good enough to help that client. Tension every time you look at your website is a sure sign that it needs a face-lift. And anxiety whenever you check your email could mean that you need to clean out that cluttered inbox.

If something's bothering you today, it's going to bother you no matter how successful you become. Stress is pointing out where the biggest gaps in your business and life exist and how to go about fixing them. If it's unproductive stress, then it's time to send those bad habits to flight because they're only holding you back from being successful. Instead of trying to avoid stress, we want to actually follow it and notice where it's pointing us. Once we deal with the stressor in the first place, we won't feel the stress anymore.

Unproductive stress will identify our limiting beliefs, unrealistic expectations, loose boundaries, or places where we're just pushing ourselves too hard. It will teach us where we need to draw the line with one particular person and where we need to delegate the work to another.

But how do we know exactly what stress is trying to tell us? How do we know if this is a situation in which we should take a stand, or if we'd be better off changing our attitudes? Stress will tell you exactly what's going on. But you have to learn how to speak its language first.

The Language of Stress

Maybe you're a stomach-clencher. Or more of a shoulder-holder. Maybe you're the nauseated type. Or that sweaty palms guy. Whatever your style, stress speaks to you in a specific way. Since early childhood, we've learned particular patterns for how we hold stress in our bodies. And, once we can translate, we can start decoding the message.

Back in my PR days, I remember getting neck stiffness before I had a major call with one particular client. When the coincidence continued on for three or four times, I knew I couldn't excuse this on sleeping funny anymore. This client was literally a *pain in my neck*. So I decided to pay attention to the neck tension and notice what other times in my life I felt it. And I noticed that I felt it every time I was afraid of being yelled at. My shoulders would rise up to my head, like an animal protecting itself from a predator.

I knew that if I wanted the stress to dissipate, I'd have to stand up to my client and set stronger boundaries. It was either that or neck pain for the rest of our interactions together. So I did what had to be done, and the strangest thing happened. Not only did the neck tension disappear, but I actually felt excited for calls with this client from then on. Without stress sending a clear-cut message, I may never have found my inner strength or have improved my relationship with that client.

Every body is different and speaks its own language. What might get one person's heart pumping will get another person's muscles to tense. The key to unlocking your own stress Rosetta Stone is to notice what's going on when you feel particularly stressed. If you feel your stomach clench right before a networking event, think about any other times that you've felt your stomach clench. Maybe you've noticed digestive issues every time you've given a presentation. Your body is telling you that this situation feels just like giving a presentation. Instead of being professional at the networking event, maybe you could relax and be yourself. Maybe you could take some pressure off. You might notice that your stomach releases, even with just that thought. The message is that your body feels stressed when you feel "on stage" instead of being authentically yourself.

So tune in and pay attention to your own body. Start to notice what your body is trying to teach you. When you learn to speak the language of your stress, you can start to use that information to improve your life. If you're stressed every time you step into your office, there's a problem there that needs to be addressed. If you feel neck strain whenever your business partner calls, there's a red flag right there. And, if you tighten your stomach or get moody right before a customer meeting, that is giving you a big clue about that relationship.

When you start to get literate in the language of stress, you can pinpoint exactly what's wrong in your life and how to fix it.

Stress Junkies

So there's productive stress, which gives you the ammo to charge forward, and unproductive stress, which gives you the messages you need to change your life. But no matter if it's friend or foe, can't we take stress too far? Can't we rely on the stress mentor a little too often? There's a reason that stress is destroying everything in its path, from our sleep cycles to our relationships. We are a culture of complete stresspots. And it's because we're addicted.

If insecurity is our social epidemic, then stress is our addiction. We crave it. Bad.

Stress keeps us moving forward. It's like an energy drink when we need a boost. We rely on it like we rely on our morning coffee. It reminds us of our never-ending task list, fuels us with motivation, and keeps us on track to accomplish more. But there can even be too much of a good thing.

Stress has become our default setting. We use the extra energy to add on more work. We can run around like madmen and fit more into our schedules. The more we do, the more we can accomplish. And the more we can accomplish, the closer to "good enough" we will be.

We're so addicted to stress that we just can't relax. We're more comfortable being stressed. Five minutes on the couch, and we immediately turn on the TV or whip out the smartphone. We think about what else we could be doing—how we should really be folding laundry, or taking out the garbage, or responding to emails. We want to feel that rush from stress. We crave that cortisol jolt. Because it makes us feel productive and worthwhile and all the other words that mean "good enough" in our culture. We don't feel worthwhile sitting in a park or lying down after a long day. We feel worthwhile when we're accomplishing more.

In a culture as fast-paced as ours, there's always more we could be doing. Every time we're on top of our to-do lists, we add a little more to our lives. We've grown to distrust downtime. It could be better spent volunteering or picking up a hobby or working longer hours. We just feel more comfortable being stressed; it's what we've always known.

And, at that rate, we couldn't possibly learn anything from stress. It's like studying all day, every day and expecting yourself to memorize everything you've learned. If we don't slow down and give ourselves time to process the messages our mentor is doling out, we'll never be able to use stress to our advantage. We can't possibly learn how to grow if we don't give ourselves space to do so. After a stressful situation, we need to sit back, reflect, and give ourselves space to learn the lesson.

The presence of stress itself isn't such a bad thing. Stress is a great way to expand beyond where we are. We feel stress when we're breaking through our fears and limiting beliefs. The problem comes when we don't stop pushing ourselves into new stressful situations. We let everyday stresses pile up, and we wonder why it feels like the world is crashing down around us.

If we're serious about creating success on our own terms, then we have to start using stress strategically. We need to pick the stress that's helping us move toward success, and dump the unnecessary stress that's just bringing us down.

To become successful, we need to start seeing stress as our mentor and paying attention to its advice. Some things are worth the fight, and some things are better to just drop and send to flight. But we have to slow down, pay attention to our bodies, and figure out exactly what stress is telling us.

And, if you can master stress, there's not much else standing in your way of success.

CHALLENGES

Complete the following challenges before moving on to the next chapter. Stress will always be present in our lives and is there for a reason, so we might as well use it to help us reach our success goals.

1. Make a list of the last five times you were stressed out. What were you stressed about? Was it productive stress that you could use to your advantage? Or was it unproductive stress that left you stuck taking no action and feeling tense? If it was productive stress, write down what it helped you to do. If it was unproductive stress, write down what message you think the stress was trying to give you and how you'll incorporate that lesson into your life.

2. Notice where you carry most of your stress in your body. Do you get clammy hands? Do you get a stiff neck? Maybe you're a shoulder-holder. Or a stomach-clencher. Take note of what that stress response means to your particular body.

   I. Now remember any times you've gotten this feeling in the recent past. What was happening? Was somebody yelling at you? Were you afraid of being rejected? Did you think you weren't capable of doing something? Start to create a stress map for yourself that matches up the way you hold stress with what it exactly means. When you understand your own stress language, you can read your own stress map.

3. Consider your main sources of stress. Are any of them needless? Could you eliminate or limit one or two of those sources, so your schedule is freer? This week, make a commitment to eliminate at least one source of stress to give yourself time and space to process the other stress and learn its message. Maybe you decide to stop checking your work email after hours. Maybe you decide to hire somebody to clean and do laundry once a week. Whatever you choose, find a way to remove one source of stress so you can more effectively use the other stress in your life.

8

It's a Long Trek. Lighten Your Load

As my practice finally started growing with opportunities abounding, I noticed that success still didn't really feel like success. I was doing what I wanted with my life, I was making good money, but I still felt weighed down. It still felt like work. My task list was sky high, but I was only really excited about one or two things. I was overcommitted all over the place. And I didn't feel the freedom I expected to come with success.

I had no boss setting my hours. No manager telling me what to do. No supervisor controlling my life. I realized that if I wasn't happy with my life, I was the one who had to change something. I had to drop anything that didn't match up with my definition of success. I had to lighten my load.

I immediately stopped anything that wasn't bringing me excitement. I cut my obligation list way down. No more marketing materials. No more speaking opportunities. No more boring networking parties.

And the decluttering process got addictive. If I was going to step up and help lead people to their own versions of success, then I'd have to really live mine out fully. I'd have to commit 100 percent. And that meant letting go of whatever was stopping me from getting there.

I said goodbye to toxic relationships. I spent less time in front of a computer and more time outside. I started taking just-for-fun classes in the middle of the day. I started working much fewer hours. And I was determined to demand success on my own terms.

I had to let go of my limiting belief that success needed to be hard work. I had to let go of my fears of having all the attention on me. Most of all, I had to let go of my conviction that I wasn't good enough to succeed exactly as I was, doing things my way.

The more I let go and peeled back the layers, the more I started to feel like myself. Nothing was holding me back anymore. This was real. I was me—all of me. And I was finally about to see just how good enough I really was.

Successful People Are Quitters

There's a myth in the success conversation. There's this idea that quitting is the antithesis of success. Inspirational posters in offices everywhere would have you believe that successful people never quit a day in their lives. That perseverance, determination, and hard work are the keys to success. That slaving away is the ultimate path to that big break.

Sure, people have climbed the success ladder on the rungs of hard work and perseverance. But they've also gotten there through quitting time and time again. In fact, quitting is one of the most critical steps to becoming successful—especially successful on your own terms. You can't reach success until you start quitting.

We're taught that quitting is disloyal and irresponsible. That it's for people who are scared, unmotivated, apathetic, lazy. We're taught that quitting is what cowards do. That the only path to success is to keep moving forward in spite of setback after setback. That we need to keep running into that wall until it finally breaks down.

But I know plenty of people who have quit their way to success. I know alcoholics who quit booze to go on to become very successful businesspeople. I know people-pleasers who quit caring what others thought to go on and create amazing and unconventional products. I know accountants who quit crunching numbers to finally create award-winning screenplays. I know friends who quit toxic relationships to go on to find true love.

In every single success story I've ever heard, quitting has been a pivotal piece of the puzzle. Without quitting, you're weighing yourself down with the extra baggage you've been carrying around.

And the journey to success has a one carry-on maximum.

The Trouble with Commitment

There are lots of reasons that hold people back from quitting. But no reason even holds a flame to the commitment excuse. Contrary to what popular chick flicks would have you believe, this culture is not that commitment-phobic. In fact, we're commitment obsessed.

We commit to everything and anything under the sun—from taking on an extra work project to helping a friend move. We seem to agree to every favor, no questions asked. And then we grow resentful when our lives feel out of control. We start to blame our to-do lists for our stressful lives. We're overburdened, depleted, exhausted. There's so much we *have to do*, and almost no time for what we *want to do*.

Now I have a bone to pick with the *have to do* culture today. We're so quick to throw blame onto everybody else. We're quick to pretend we have no control over our lives. Think of all of the times in a day that you say you "have to do" something. We *have to* go to work, do the dishes, see that friend, visit our mother. The list could go on and on. In fact, I'd argue that the majority of our days are spent on the *have tos*.

In reality, there's nothing we *have to do*. But there's a heck of a lot that we *choose to do*. We have a choice in the matter. We have a say over everything we do. We may choose to go to work, or else we risk getting fired. But that's a choice we're making. Our own choice. We can get fired all we want. Or we can be seen as irresponsible. Or we can take a personal day if we feel the need. All of it is a choice, regardless of what we feel we *have to do*.

The problem with commitment is that we attach ourselves to some person, event, or activity. We become a part of it. And we forget there ever was or is a choice involved. It becomes another *have to*, another task on the list, another obligation to fulfill. But we have a choice. There's always a choice. And, if you aren't fired up by your commitment anymore, you might be hitching yourself to the wrong wagon.

We're afraid of breaking commitments because it would only reinforce the belief that we're unreliable, useless, not good enough. Maybe if we take on the whole world, we'll be important and special and needed. Maybe then people will see how worthwhile we are. Maybe they'll even come to respect and rely on us. It really doesn't get any more "worth it" than being relied upon.

But breaking commitments is part of the journey to becoming a good quitter. And we've already established that you've got to be a good quitter to get successful—at least the kind of successful that you want.

So start saying "no." Start turning down offers and obligations. Get comfortable disappointing people. Get okay with shutting off that phone or powering down that email. Stop making commitments and start politely breaking the ones that no longer serve you.

You can't waste all of your energy on commitments that are holding you back. Because this is your journey to success. And you're going to need all the energy you can get to make it there.

Your Life Is the Sum of its Parts

It's been years since I've taken algebra, but I do remember that when you want to know what something amounts to, you have add it up—with all of the positives and negatives. If you want to know what your life amounts to, you have to add that up too—with all of *its* positives and negatives. Some things bring you up and some things bring you down. That's just life.

Do you notice how you're in a great mood after you finally get to catch up with your best friend? Or how walking into your home is so calming and relaxing? But those phone calls with your coworker always drain you. And even thinking about walking into that mess of a basement stresses you out.

We've all got positives and negatives in our lives. Things that give us energy and things that suck the life out of us. People who support us, nourish us, make us feel like we can accomplish the world. Others who judge, criticize, and nitpick everything we do. We've got good behaviors, like exercising in the morning and staying in to rest on Friday nights. Or bad ones, like grabbing that quick cigarette when we're stressed or giving in too easily when people disagree with us. We're a combination of positives and negatives, and the sum of that combination determines what our life amounts to. It determines how successful we are. It determines how much we love our lives.

There are two ways to make your life more positive: you can add in more positive things, or you can reduce the negatives. Now, I don't know about you, but I'm pretty filled to the brim already. Between work and relationships and household chores and some semblance of a social life, I've got a lot going on. I can't fit a ton more into my life unless I let go of some things.

Anything negative in your life is holding you back from loving your life completely. It's bringing you down, lowering your value, reducing what your life amounts to. If you want to have a positive life, you've got to get rid of the negative aspects.

Call it a life declutter or some personal feng shui. By dropping the dead weight, you're automatically making your life more positive *and* you're making room for more positivity in your life. As you start to let go of what's only hurting, you can add in more things that will help.

Maybe it's as simple as limiting your time with that one negative friend. Or it could be kicking that bad habit of eating chocolate when you're stressed. Maybe it's more of a toxic relationship that needs ending. Or it could even be breaking your pattern of always becoming a control freak when you're scared.

We've all got our dirty little habits that bring us down. They hold us back from ever achieving the level of success that we fantasize about. Because, when we travel toward success, all of us is going. The good, the bad, and the ugly. The sum of our lives. And you can't fly toward success if you're being weighed down by negativity.

When you lighten your load, that's when you see how high you can really soar.

Self-Care or Just Plain Selfish?

Anything that challenges us is going to be hard. If it challenges our core beliefs, it's even harder. And the idea that quitting can propel you forward on your path to success is a lot to swallow. So, if you're feeling some resistance come up here, join the club.

Quitting anything, saying no, and being selfish are all looked down upon in our culture. They're icky, they're uncomfortable, and they bring up a lot of feelings of self-entitlement and self-indulgence. Doesn't it seem like any word with the prefix "self" is automatically over-the-top? It's like any time we spend a little bit of extra love and attention on ourselves, we're cast out as egotistical and greedy.

We feel like we have an obligation to our work, or to our families, or to our friends, or to our communities. And, if we put ourselves before them, even for a second, then we're just plain selfish. We need to be there at all hours. The world will collapse if we aren't saving the day.

Hate to break it to you, sugar, but you're just not that important.

We're so desperate to be perceived as important, most of all to ourselves, that we're willing to put up with even the most toxic behaviors and draining activities. We pretend we can't take five minutes for ourselves. We pretend we have to put up with grueling conditions. We pretend that it's better to sacrifice our own happiness for the betterment of others.

That's not altruism. That's low self-esteem.

Self-care is like a pail of water. You can't help other people's pails unless yours is already filled up. It's about feeding yourself the stuff that you need. Nourishing yourself with what fuels your success. It's simple, really. Give yourself the foods that make you feel good, hang out with the people who support you, surround yourself with activities that light you up, and limit the junk that makes you feel like crap.

When we're really honest with ourselves, we can admit that we have a few detrimental behaviors we could drop. We have a few toxic relationships that could use some revamping. We have a bit of clutter that could use dumping. We have to clear away the junk to let our real selves shine through.

As it turns out, self-care really just means taking care of yourself so that you can be more effective at life. If you aren't willing to treat yourself like a success, who will?

How Do You Know When Enough Is Enough?

But the fact of the matter remains that sometimes quitting really is just giving up because you're scared or frustrated or not willing to push forward. Sometimes quitting is really about not putting in the extra effort to get what you want. So how do you know when you're quitting for good or quitting for evil, so to speak?

Way back at the beginning, what might feel like ages ago now, we put together our own personal definition of success. Not what our Aunt Alice said. Not even what our grandmother said. What we said.

And, in that definition, we were pretty clear on what we wanted out of life. The big picture stuff. All the things that made us feel happy and strong and successful. We didn't need to get into the nitpicky details because the vision was really clear. Things either matched up to that definition or they didn't. They either helped you move toward success or away from it. There was no in between.

That, my friends, is how you know when enough is enough. That's how you know if it's something to quit or time to keep chugging along. It's either bringing you to your definition of success or it's not.

Too often, we confuse the process with the result. We get so caught up in the day-to-day of what we're doing that we lose sight of the big picture. We get so caught up in *what* we're doing that we forget *why* we're doing it. It's like the businessman who works hard to buy a nice summer house for his family but can never take off work to get down there. Or the writer who desperately wants to publish a book but gets so caught up in the perfect wording that she can't get it done.

Sure, things come up in the middle. You get lost in the woods of the work and there's no end in sight. But it's times like this that you need to hone back in on the big picture. Why are you struggling through this to begin with?

If it's something that's bringing you toward your definition of success, absolutely keep it up. If it's taking you further from where you want to be, back it up and haul outta there. And, if you're not really sure either way, see if you can trade it in for something better that you *do know* is bringing you to where you want to be.

Your definition of success should invigorate you. It should excite you. It should make you feel more like yourself than you ever knew possible. Even if you're scared, even if you're frustrated—you should still have this sense of hope and excitement. That's how you know you're moving in the right direction.

If it's not that, then it might be time to quit.

Your preferences will change. What once invigorated you might one day become toxic. You'll grow, you'll evolve, you'll transform. And so too will the things you want to quit. But you're not tied to your commitments from the past. At any moment, you have the ability to choose the best and most nourishing things for yourself. At any moment, you have the ability to quit anything that is burdening you or tying you down.

Quitters are in control of their lives. They're people who decide what's best for them at any given moment. And that's what makes them so successful.

CHALLENGES

Complete the following challenges before moving on to the next chapter. Unhealthy and unnecessary thoughts, beliefs, behaviors, and relationships are holding you back from achieving the level of success that you deserve. When you let go of what no longer helps you, you make room for new opportunities.

1. Make a list of everything you do in a typical day. Next to each item, write +1 for things you like, +2 for things you really like, and +3 for things you absolutely love. For the less than ideal things, write -1 for things you dislike, -2 for things you can't stand, and -3 for the things you hate most. Now add up your list. Are you positive or negative? This represents how positive you think your days are. Add a few of these days together, and it represents how positive you think your life is.

   I. Now go through the list and see if there's any of the negative stuff that you can eliminate or minimize (especially the -3 stuff). The more negatives that you can eliminate, the more room you make for new positives in your life.

2. Make a list of every commitment you have in your life. For example, you commit to showing up to work everyday. Or you commit to sending out newsletters for your company. Or you commit to doing laundry twice a week. Or you commit to making dinner every other

day. Whatever your commitments, throw them all on the list. Now look at how much you've committed yourself to. It's probably a really long list.

I. How much of that list still excites you? How many things do you love doing? How much of it feels natural to you? How much pumps you up and gives you energy?

II. If there are any commitments that no longer excite you, they're draining you of energy. Drop as many commitments as possible. For the ones that you can't drop, see if there's a way for you to make them more exciting. Maybe put on some music and dance while you're doing the dishes. Or maybe you could listen to an audiobook while you enter your expenses into a spreadsheet. The point is to turn all *have tos* into *want tos* so your life looks exactly as successful as you want it to.

3. Think about your definition of success from Chapter 1. What toxic behaviors and beliefs do you need to quit to become as successful as your definition? Maybe part of your successful definition was to eat healthier. Could you drop the fried food from your diet? Or maybe success to you is valuing your time more. Could you cut Facebook out between 9 a.m. and 5 p.m.? Give yourself permission to quit anything that's holding you back from success.

9

Learn How to Enjoy Every Moment

I'll never forget the day that I reached one hundred blog subscribers. One hundred people wanted to hear what I had to say every day. One hundred people read my words over their morning coffees. I felt like I was really making a difference in people's lives. I felt like I had really made it.

But, shortly after, one hundred sounded miniscule. I was in business and mastermind groups where members boasted 100,000 subscribers. All I had was one hundred. I felt the shame of being a nobody. I stopped calling myself a blogger. I'd have to work harder and achieve more to earn that title.

Fortunately, I surround myself with people a lot smarter than I am. It's one of my shortcuts to success. And one of those brilliant people caught me in the midst of one of those narcissistic meltdowns that only entrepreneurs and creatives can understand.

He looked at me point-blank and said, "You said you just wanted to change one life. Based on your fan emails, you've changed a lot more than that. At what point will you let yourself enjoy success?"

And there it hit me. All at once. It's not about how much success you can achieve; it's about how much success you can enjoy. It's not a destination at all, but a journey to happiness. And, if you can't let happiness in now, you'll never reach it—no matter how "successful" you become.

I thought back to that day that I reached one hundred blog subscribers. Few people have ever felt as successful. I was on top of the world. I was doing what I loved, I was helping people, and I was making money. There wasn't much more I needed.

I had a decision to make right then and there. Either I could choose to savor every moment of success, or I could choose to keep striving to ever feel successful enough.

In that, and every other moment since, I chose success.

The Story of the Bottomless Bucket

Back when I was in college, I took a class on wellness. I figured it was an easy A during my last semester. How much would I really have to do in a class called wellness?

When I walked in on the first day, I saw a bunch of buckets, shovels, and sand. The teacher instructed us to fill the buckets up with sand. When we were done, we just had to lift it up and show her that it was full, and then we'd get an A on the assignment. Seemed simple enough. I was right. Wellness was a joke.

I decided to be the first to finish, true to my nature. I skipped the whole shoveling process and proceeded to pour the bag of sand right into the bucket. There. First done. In only a few seconds.

I called the teacher over proudly. She smiled and asked me to hold the bucket up for her to inspect. Just as I did, I noticed a small trail of sand traveling from the bucket down onto my desk. I looked under the bucket to find a small hole letting all of my sand right out.

She smiled at my realization and said softly, "I guess you better plug that hole before you put any more sand in. No amount of sand in the world can fill a bottomless bucket."

With one simple exercise, in the first five minutes of class, I learned more about life than I ever did in any calculus class. At its very root, our *not good enough* culture has almost nothing to do with how much we can achieve, and almost everything to do with how much we can accept.

Try telling a woman with anorexia that she's thin, and your words will fall on deaf ears. Try telling a self-deprecating man that he's handsome, and he'll scoff it off. No amount of compliments will ever be able to fill up their self-esteem. Because there is a hole in their bucket, and all of those compliments just slip right on through.

Our buckets are our containers for what we'll allow into our lives. They contain everything from the money we're willing to receive, to the amount of love we think we deserve, to the success we'll let ourselves enjoy. If there's a hole or crack in any place, then we're going to start leaking out. But the modern solution to our bottomless buckets is to keep adding more. We work longer hours, strive for more promotions, pine away for more money.

We think that if we can just reach that next milestone—six-figure salary or partner status or twenty clients—then we'll be successful. Then our bucket will finally be filled. So we add and add and add. But, no matter what we add, it just seems to slip right past us. It never seems enough. Because we never feel enough. It's almost a comedy routine à la *The Three Stooges*. We fill and watch it leak out. Then fill and watch it leak out.

But what if we did as my teacher said and plugged that hole? What if, instead of adding and adding, we just fixed the hole in the first place? We'd probably need to add in a lot less. We'd probably have a full bucket with much less work.

I call self-esteem the "enough bucket" because it's a good gauge of how *enough* we feel. When we use statements like "I'm not smart enough," or "I'm not rich enough," it means we have a hole in our self-esteem. We'll never be able to spill our fortune over to anyone else because we always have a hole in our own bucket. We'll never do anything for the greater good or live out our deepest passions if we have a hole. Because, deep down, all we're ever trying to do is fill up our self-esteem. And, secretly, behind everything we do is that desire to achieve until we're good enough. Until we have a full bucket.

Your Success Can Only Climb as High as Your Worth

Do you ever notice that people stay at just about the same level of happiness, regardless of what's going on in their lives? I know some people who just can't seem to be happy, no matter how good things get. They say they want more money, but the raise never seems high enough. They say they want more romance, but they can't pull themselves away from work. It's like they're determined to be miserable.

Either that or they've reached their limit of self-worth.

We've all set the bar for about what we think we deserve in this world. From an early age, we sized ourselves up to the competition and decided exactly what we're worth. It's the price tag we put on ourselves. It spells out what kind of love we should get, how we should be treated, what kind of job we should work, how much money we should make, how happy we should be, and so on. It spells out exactly how much success we're willing to accept.

If we cross over that limit, we'll shoot ourselves back down. Our bucket is only comfortable being full to the extent that we think we're worth. If it gets fuller, we engage in the age-old art of self-sabotage. We find ways to leak the excess out of the bucket so we can be right back where we think we deserve to be.

How often do lottery ticket winners end up back where they started? How often does that opportunity that "you can't believe happened" suddenly fall through? We end relationships that are going too well. We start problems because we can't stand complacency. We master one big accomplishment and plunge ourselves right into the next. We bring ourselves back to the exact level of happiness that we'll allow ourselves.

But, most of the time, we don't even get to the self-sabotage stage. We pre-select ourselves for everything in our lives. We only apply to the jobs that we think we deserve. We only ask out the people who we think will say yes. We ask for just as much money as we think we're worth. We put up with about just as much abuse in relationships as we think we have to.

Only we don't see it as a self-worth thing. We see it as a "just the way things are" thing. We claim we have to stay in our toxic job because it's a bad economy. We claim we can't ask that girl out because she's superficial and only dates rich men. We claim we can't ask for a raise because the company just went through a rebrand. Really, we can rationalize anything if we try hard enough.

But the truth is that we can't climb higher than we've given ourselves permission to. We can't be any more successful than we've made up our minds to be. We can't allow ourselves to be happier than we think we deserve to be. And so we rationalize or make excuses or come up with all of these self-sabotaging reasons for why our lives are exactly where they are.

We're exactly where we are because that's what we think we deserve. At any moment, we can choose success. We don't need anyone else's permission. All we need is ourselves—ourselves to admit that we deserve it. That we're not going to settle this time. That we're holding out for the big time. That we're going to climb higher than we ever have before. Because we're worth it.

Buy Yourself a Pair of Rose-Colored Glasses

Years ago, my good friend Kate told me a college story of her own. She had a pair of pink and red aviator sunglasses. She called them her rose-colored glasses. And they were magical.

When she put them on, the world changed. She was confident. She was charismatic. And she could only see the positive in the world.

With her sunglasses, Kate could approach any guy in the bar. She was wittier and more courageous than anyone else around. No one could say a bad thing about her; it'd just roll off her shoulders. Because she was cool. She was a bad ass with her magical sunglasses.

People were nicer to her when she wore her sunglasses. Good luck always seemed to fall into her lap. Bad things hardly ever happened to her. And, above all, she always felt successful. Whether she was busting out some sweet moves on a sweaty dance floor or rocking it at a game of horse-shoes, she always felt successful. In her rose-colored glasses.

I always laughed at that story. How silly it was that a pair of sunglasses could suddenly change her and how she saw the world. That something as simple as a new lens could completely change her life.

Until I realized that a lens is all we've got.

On any given day, we encounter trillions of experiences. Everything from having a conversation with your friend to tying your shoes counts. But we've got to make sense of it all. We've got to put it together into some form that we can understand. So we develop a story—a story about our lives.

You could go to work, have a stressful meeting, get stuck in traffic on your way home, and get rear-ended and have to deal with insurance. You might call that a bad day. If it happens often enough, you might call that a bad life. Or you could be grateful for having a well-paying job, meetings that challenge you, transportation to and from work, and not having been hurt in an accident. Same exact circumstances, different story. And it's all about the lens you're wearing.

We come at life with a whole series of biases, past experiences, and preconceived notions. We start looking for experiences to validate what we already believe, rather than going into experiences fresh and new. With all of the theories and beliefs and new information out there, we have to pre-determine the way we see the world, or else it would just be overwhelming. We need to create a filter that's going to help us interpret life. We need to create a lens.

Take the news for example. How many people do you know who will only watch either Fox News or MSNBC?

We want our news to be framed in a particular way that makes sense to us. Otherwise, we'd have to throw out our entire belief system and start from scratch. And that's terrifying. How could we possibly make sense of the world if we didn't have some lens to look at it through?

But that's all it is. A lens. A perspective. A viewpoint on how things are going in your life. You could choose to see everything that's going on with you as success or as failure. You could choose to see your job as a life-sucking wasteland or a place that provides you with money. You could see your unemployment as a death sentence or as an opportunity to figure out your next move.

On their own, none of these mean a heck of a lot. You've got to apply your filter to make sense of them. And, if your lens isn't working out too well for you, pick up another pair.

We construct our meaning of the world through the stories we tell ourselves. If we don't like what's going on in our lives, we just have to change the story. If we don't feel successful yet, we just have to put on a new pair of glasses. We just have to look at our lives from a new perspective. We just have to see the world with fresh eyes.

We've got the ability—we've all got the ability—to wear magical sunglasses. At any moment, we can put on the proverbial shades and suddenly become invincible. We can start embracing freedom. We can start reveling in our successes. We can savor and enjoy every little moment. All we have to do is give ourselves permission.

Life Is Lived Moment to Moment, and Every Moment Is New

With a sturdy bucket, some sweet shades, and a little bit higher self-worth, I can't think of many places more appropriate to go than the beach.

There's something really magical about the beach, isn't there? Something really special. Feeling the sand beneath my toes, the wind rustling through my hair, and the cool splash of water on my face, I have a really hard time remembering what stress and anxiety feel like.

I start every single year at the beach. I go to Aruba for New Year's Eve and start the year with some fresh ocean breeze. And the funny thing is, no matter what's happening in my life, I usually forget all about it. I've gone to the beach after losing my passport and quitting my job and making cringe-worthy mistakes and breaking my heart and overcoming a life-changing sickness. And the sea is just waiting for me, calm as ever. Like nothing else matters.

Nothing is guaranteed. Nothing is permanent. Not even our super-secure job. Not even our next breath. We don't know what the future will hold. And, for all the planning and strategizing and really smart work that we do, we might be thrown for a complete loop. Nothing is for sure except this moment. This one moment in time.

The beach reminds me of that.

Life isn't a résumé. Success isn't a set of accomplishments. It's moments—a whole string of moments—that make up a happy life. We don't know what tomorrow will bring or what will even happen in five minutes. But we can savor this one moment. We can let ourselves enjoy the touch of a loved one, or the taste of a delicious meal, or the sheer joy we brought a client, or even the sand beneath our feet.

Instead of rushing from one achievement to the next, like a marathon runner checks off each mile, we can slow down for a second. We can notice each moment as it passes. We can let ourselves feel proud of something—even as small as reading this chapter and taking a step toward success. We can remember how fortunate we are. We can feel gratitude toward our life. We can love what we've accomplished. And a whole string of those feelings makes a pretty successful life.

If we never feel success, we'll never be successful. It's not a destination. It's a feeling. It's acknowledgement that this moment feels good. And you're proud of how you're living it. And the future might be different, but right now is successful.

And that's something to savor.

CHALLENGES

Complete the following challenges before moving on to the next chapter. Success is not achieved at a certain milestone; it is lived in individual moments. If we want to be successful, we need to choose success in each and every moment.

1. Think about your life as a whole. What aspects never seem to be fulfilled? No matter how hard you try, you can never satisfy that part of your life. Maybe your love life is MIA. Or maybe you seem to be struggling financially. Maybe you've always battled with your weight. Or you lack confidence in yourself.

   I. The aspect that can never be filled is where you have a hole in your bucket. It's an area in which you are not satisfied with yourself. No matter what comes into your life, you either don't accept it or don't appreciate it because you don't think that you deserve it.

   II. Instead of looking outside of yourself to fill the bucket up with more stuff, look inside to plug that hole. How can you learn to be happy and satisfied with yourself as you are in this very moment? If the problem is your love life, then maybe you need to start taking yourself out on romantic self-dates to show yourself just how much you're worth. If the problem is your financial life, then maybe you need to hire a finance coach or talk to an accountant about how to get your affairs in order. When you start plugging the holes in your bucket, you allow yourself to be satisfied with what you've got and set yourself up to attract more.

3. On a piece of paper, write down how much money you currently make per year. Now, under it, be honest with yourself and write down exactly how much money you think you deserve to make per year. Look at that number and sit with it. How does it feel?

   I. Finally, double the number that you think you deserve. How does that feel? What emotions come up? Do you think you deserve it? Double it again. What comes up now? Is there excitement? Fear? Doubt? Is there a little voice in the back of your mind? Notice the stories you tell yourself about what you deserve.

4. Write out all the events that happened to you today. Jot down everything from hitting the snooze button in the morning to the long commute home at night. Throw it all down there on paper. This is your story of your day. This is how you see your life.

   I. Now put on your rose-colored glasses. Give yourself permission to see your life in a new light. How would you retell the same story with the same facts to make it successful? Did you get to go to a job where you made good money? Did you get to see family or friends? Did you work on something you were passionate about? Did you have a special moment?

II. Notice how the same facts can tell a very different story, depending on how you look at it.

5. Give yourself permission to savor moments of success this week. It can be anything that you define as successful. You could have a moment to catch the sunset on your commute home from work. You could make a sale and decide to take yourself out for an ice cream. You could surprise your loved one with a special present just because you've successfully stayed together this long.

I. Instead of planning ahead and plotting your next move, give yourself permission to just be in the moment. Allow yourself to feel the success of this moment.

10

You Can't Please Everyone, So Stop Trying

Growing up, I was a lot to handle. I would spill over my glass of water at the dinner table. I would get yelled at for being louder than any of the other students in class. Sometimes I couldn't control the sound of my voice. Sometimes I couldn't stop my hands from waving around madly while I talked. I was passionate, vibrant, excited.

Regularly, people told me that I was *too much*. In fact, in one of my first jobs, my boss sat me down and said, "Your work is amazing, but your personality was a little too much. You were too excited and playful at first. But, once you toned it down, you started fitting in."

I was a lot to handle. I was too full of life. And I so badly wanted to fit in. So I learned to tone it down and tighten it up to fit in with the rest of the world. I learned how to stop being who I was and started being what people wanted. Because I could definitely change myself into a successful person.

But somewhere along my success journey, I realized that I didn't want to be someone else to be successful. I wanted to be successful as myself. This was success on my terms, and I wanted to be successful exactly as I am.

I didn't want to tone it down anymore. I wanted to crank up the volume. I wanted to passionately yell about health-care reform and then dance around my living room wildly. I wanted to whip people into their most successful selves and then excitedly talk about my newest herbs.

It occurred to me that maybe I wasn't *too much*. Maybe it was that other people just couldn't keep up with me. They weren't the right fits. And the more I was myself, the more I let the ideal clients, friends, and relationships into my life. People were looking for me all along, but they couldn't find me because I was toning myself down. Not everyone was a fit, but the ones who were wanted the *too much* version of me.

In a culture where we never feel like *enough*, we certainly chastise people for being *too much*. But I realized that I'm neither *not enough* nor *too much*. I'm just me. I'm just Mike who's happy and vibrant and excited. And, if people wanted to be a part of that, that's great. If they didn't, that's great too. But I wasn't going to change who I am either way.

So I decided to be myself, whether people liked it or not. I decided to really create success on my own terms.

The Art of Disappointing

There are over seven billion people in the world. If wars are any indication, the odds of getting all seven billion of them to agree on anything are very, very slim. Whether we like it or not, chances are one or two people might disagree with us from time-to-time. That's just a fact of life. So why are we all so afraid of that?

We censor ourselves to prevent offending anyone. We hold ourselves back because we fear rejection. We tweak and modify and tone down everything to make it perfect for the audience we're speaking to. We mold ourselves to fit everyone around us. Because, if everyone likes us, then we're automatically successful. Successful people are liked by the world, right?

Wrong!

Disappointing people is one of the sure-fire signs that you're on the path to success. In fact, the more strongly you can make people feel about you—good or bad—the more successful you can become.

Think about celebrities. You probably have a few whom you love. You probably have a few whom you can't stand, too. But the ones that come to the top of your mind are usually on one extreme end or the other. Nobody remembers the middle ground. Nobody remembers the moderate guy. We remember those who have a strong presence. We remember the people who take a strong stance.

I'll let you in on a little secret at this point: your version of success, whatever it is to you, is intricately tied up with self-acceptance. What you want out of life is wholly unique. It represents who you are: your talents, your goals, your desires. The kind of stuff that nobody can really copy.

So, if you're playing the safe bet and not disappointing anyone, then you can't possibly be living out your own definition of success. Because you're not being yourself strongly enough. You're not being unique or interesting or adventurous. You're playing by somebody else's rules. You're adopting his or her definition of success. And I thought we agreed to give up on that in Chapter 1.

Disappointing people is an art. And, like all good art forms, it takes practice. You're not just going to read this chapter and magically get really good at disappointing people. You're not just going to stop caring what people think because you suddenly decided to. You have to practice. You have to start letting people down. You have to change your mentality from *living for others* to *living for yourself.* You have to feel the sweaty palms and racing heartbeat and shortness of breath, and know that the storm will pass.

You have to decide that other people are great. But this is your journey. This is your life. And your opinion is most important.

And Then You Sweep the Rug from under Them

Will there be backlash? Will there be struggles? Will there be a colossal meltdown? You betcha. That's what happens when you change the rules.

Think of it this way: you make rules for your game of life. For the hell of it, let's call those boundaries. You set boundaries and teach people how to treat you. You let them know that phone calls after 8 p.m. are okay or that you'll respond to emails while on vacation. You make it clear that you're always available to be a shoulder to cry on or to drop everything and attend to them. You establish the rules for engagement.

And then—*boom!*—you sweep the rug out from under them. You change the rules in the middle of the game. And, as a competitive board-gamer myself, I can tell you that changing the rules at halftime just doesn't fly.

We put people in boxes. We give them assigned roles. We know that Susie is the one we call when we have work troubles, and Matt is the friend for really bad days. We know that Jessica will drop everything when we need a night out, and that Dave is good for a game of golf. Since we first met, we put the contract in place. This is how things are. This is how they've always been.

So, if one of those friends were to up and neglect the duties, we'd be mad. We'd be furious. We'd see it as a personal attack on us. We'd think that they were being selfish. Catch my drift?

Renegotiating relationships is a tricky business because you're not only changing your own life; you're changing other people's. And then come the insecurities—the fears that you're improving your life and leaving them in the dust. The idea that your actions are making a personal judgment about their way of life. The reminder that they're sitting home eating junk food, while you're hitting the gym every day. Before, you were partners in sloth, but now—*Et tu, Brute?*

Don't be shocked if you face some undue anger or resentment. Change is hard. When it feels unprompted, it's even harder. The moments when we need the most support are often when it's the furthest away. Because we're rebalancing the scale. We're recalibrating. And that takes some adjusting—for us and for everyone around us.

Slow down. Be easy on yourself. Find other resources for support. Find people who are going through similar circumstances. Trust in yourself. And know that you are re-establishing life on your own terms. Probably for the first time ever.

A Lesson in Humility

With all the potential backlash, it's no wonder we're afraid to disappoint people. So I've found that the secret to getting really good at letting people down is to eat a healthy slice of some humble pie.

A few years ago, I was traveling around Israel with a group of people, including a few days with five Israeli soldiers. We spent days and nights together, so we all got pretty close. We laughed about our differences, bonded over our similarities, and discussed everything from life and love to the latest celebrity scandal.

When the trip was coming to an end, the soldiers surprised us at the airport—having traveled from all over the country just to meet back up and say goodbye. They brought us gifts and thanked us for a great trip. But, one of the soldiers, Tal, whom I had gotten very close with, did something completely unexpected. He took off his dog tags right there in the airport in front of everyone and handed them to me. He caught the confused look on my face and simply responded, "I wanted to give you the most personal thing I could think of. Because you changed my life."

I'll never forget the shock I felt at that moment. I couldn't believe his words. My mind quickly raced over the entire five days we had spent together. I couldn't remember one insightful thing I had said. I couldn't remember one helpful comment I had made. I couldn't even remember any moment that I had tried to help him.

And that's when I understood humility. It isn't about a polite statement you make when you accept an award. It isn't about being shy or unassuming. It isn't even about the feeling you get when you're grateful. It's about the fact that, in reality, we have no control. We have no say over what people will say or think or do. We don't know what will affect people—what will really affect people—because we aren't them.

We may have the best plan in the world. We may execute it perfectly, and it just might not fly. Because it's not our decision to make. It's not even ours to begin with. It's just a talent, a skill, a gift we have. And we never know how it's going to affect people.

I thought about that story when I started writing this chapter. I thought about my own struggles with peo-ple-pleasing. (It never really ends; you just get a little bit better with it.) I want people to like this book, of course. I want people to say nice things about me and for nobody to criticize it. But then I remember that story. I remember humility. And I remember that it's not really in my control what people think. It's not really my business either.

We all just have to put our best foot forward and do the work that we think is right. We just have to keep marching on to the beat of our drum. Sometimes it's going to be amazing; sometimes it's not. But it's not really up to us to decide. We don't really know, anyway. It's just up to us to keep moving forward. To keep sharing our gifts with the world. And to hope that we can help a few people.

All we can do is show up. Humbled. Grateful that we get another day to use our skills to the fullest. And hope that it's helpful for somebody.

When you realize that you have no control in the first place, it makes it a lot easier to stop trying to please people. Because you honestly don't know what will really affect them anyway. You have no idea how they'll react. All you can do is share what you've got as vulnerably as possible and hope for the best.

If You Want to Attract People, You Have to Be Willing to Repel Some First

But humbled or not, the point of success isn't to disappoint and dissuade everybody, right? To be successful in any way, you have to attract some people into your life.

All the time, I get asked by clients how to attract people of their own. From new friends to lovers to customers to investors, they want to know why they aren't attracting new people. And the answer is always the same—no matter who you're trying to attract, there's only really one way to do it. To attract people, you have to be willing to repel them first.

I remember when I first started my business. I took everything personally. But I took few things as personally as when someone "un-Liked" my Facebook page. I couldn't understand it. I was furious. I was putting out better and better content, and then more people were unsubscribing. It seemed like every time I wrote something that I thought just nailed it out of the park, I'd get a mass exodus.

But something really strange was happening on the page itself. Engagement was skyrocketing. Fans were sharing my posts like never before. And more people than ever were signing on as clients. I was literally repelling my way to success.

The more I showed myself, the stronger reactions people had about me. Some people knew that I was a wrong fit and disappeared. Others felt more strongly than ever that I was the right fit for them and started hiring me. But, either way, people started to take action. I've learned that strong reactions can only happen to a strong presence.

Business and life are gambles. If we buy into the fact that we have no real control and have to be humble (hint: we do), then we don't really know what's going to attract people. We have to take risks. We have to step outside of the box.

We have to be ourselves. And that probably means repelling people. A lot of the time.

Successful people don't grasp at straws. They don't work with anyone they can get their hands on. They work with the right fits. They whittle down the seven billion people in this world into the small following that gets them. They pass on the so-so choices to find the right choices.

For better or worse, successful people are always themselves, even if that means disappointing or repelling some people.

You Need People to Succeed, but You Need Yourself More

The second we even mention the word "success," people come out of the woodwork to tell us the best way to do it. Everybody's got an opinion on the best way to attract more clients into your business or on the must-dos for snagging your ideal relationship. It seems like, around every corner, there's another expert on productivity, relationships, or success who can teach us all the best way to do it. And their advice is usually great. Their advice is incredibly helpful. If my home library is any indication, I'm a big believer in learning from people who came before me.

But the truth is that they don't know you better than you know yourself. This is your own definition of success, remember? This is on your own terms. Your exact success has never existed before. So nobody knows it like you do.

It's easy to get caught up in the advice of so-called experts. It's easy to model your efforts after the tried-and-true approaches of the past. But these approaches might not be right for you. Maybe experts advise you to write your blogs with search engine optimization in mind, when you feel more comfortable writing from the heart. Or maybe you've been told to take advantage of social media, when face-to-face interactions feel more your style.

In our own model of success, there are no rules. Actually, there is one rule: it has to feel right to you. You have to bring yourself to the table in all of your flaw-ridden, imperfect glory. You have to be too loud or too aggressive. You have to be too vulnerable or too honest. You have to yell from the rooftops exactly who you are and what you've got to offer, even if it means disappointing or upsetting some people.

If you don't factor yourself into the equation, success will never feel like success. Because it will never feel like you.

Absolutely take people's advice along your path. Absolutely take any help you can get. But, when it comes down to it, you've got to check in with yourself first and foremost and make sure this feels like you.

Everything you do, from how you build a business, to the workout routine you choose, to even finding the love of your life, has to feel right to you. We've all seen how awkward a person looks when he's trying to be someone he's not. It feels painful. It feels unnatural. And it most definitely doesn't feel successful.

We need to create a version of success with us in it. Whether we disappoint people or not, it needs to look and feel natural to us. We can listen to everybody's advice all day long. But, at the end of the day, nobody else knows how to create success for us. Only we can create the type of success that is going to make us undeniably happy. Only we know how to create success on our own terms.

CHALLENGES

Complete the following challenges before moving on to the next chapter. To be successful on your own terms, you have to be yourself. Some people may like it, and some may hate it. But this is your version of success, not anybody else's.

1. Think back over the past twenty-four hours. Write down any instances in which you held yourself back for fear of upsetting somebody else. Maybe you toned down your blog post to seem less controversial. Maybe you skipped the bright yellow T-shirt because people might have laughed at you. Maybe you choked back your political opinion because you didn't want to be judged. Notice how many times in the past twenty-four hours you changed who you were to please other people.

2. Pick one of your success goals that you feel stuck on. Write down how you think people would react if you pursued that goal. Do you think they would laugh at you? Do you think they would criticize you? Do you think they would judge you negatively?

   I. Now, imagine your most supportive, closest friend. If everybody were as supportive of you as your best friend, would you be more likely to pursue that goal? Start to recognize how your fear of others' opinions is holding you back from achieving success.

3. Make a commitment to doing something really honest and authentic this week, even if it means disappointing

people. You might tell your company that you can't stay late because you have dinner plans. You might write a heart-wrenchingly vulnerable blog post, which has the potential to turn people off. You might even back out of dinner plans so you can enjoy a night alone. Whatever you choose, do something entirely for yourself and remind yourself that you are not responsible for making anyone else happy.

4. Think of your favorite skill—whether you're a painter or a writer or a brilliant salesman or a product developer. Imagine that this skill will be taken away from you forever in one week. You will never again have the opportunity to use it after the week is up. How would you spend your week? Would you be concerned with how many people like your work? Would you stress out about what clients think about your skill? You only have so many more opportunities to use it before it dries up.

   I. Humility is about understanding that your gifts aren't yours to own. One day you could shatter your arm or have brain damage or become paralyzed, and you would never be able to use your skill again. Don't waste time worried what the result of your work might be. Use your skills while you've still got them. You are only responsible for the process, and the result is out of your control anyway.

11

Be Open to Whatever Comes Along

In my early twenties, I didn't have the strictest morals when it came to dating. I liked to party and I liked to have sex with women. It didn't really matter if they were friends or girls I had just met. I just liked to date around and have sex.

But then I got really sick. And vomiting blood kind of gets in the way of meeting girls at a bar. So I stayed home on the couch in pain. And my roommate Garrett, a good friend of mine, took pity on me. He'd stay in on Friday nights to watch movies with me or clean up my blood when I got sick. He'd go to the pharmacy to get my medicine or drive me around to all of my appointments. He'd make me laugh when I was crying. He'd rub my back when I was bent over in pain.

About two months into this routine, it occurred to me that I was in love with him. I hadn't been attracted to a man before this—at least not to my knowledge. But there I was. In love with a man.

At first, I tried to brush it off. I tried to fight it. It didn't make much sense. And I couldn't wrap my head around it. He was my best friend. I had known him for six or seven years. I had never been attracted to him before. But something had changed.

My options were clear. I could go on loving him and not doing anything about it, which seemed like a reasonable thing to do. Maybe it would pass. Maybe I was just feeling grateful for all he did for me. Or I could pursue the other option. I could tear down the only identity I knew, to both myself and others. I could step into the darkness with no light to guide me. I could let go of all the attachments to the life I thought I knew and just open up to whatever headed my way.

There's a kind of liberation that comes along with being afraid you might die. There's a kind of fearlessness that just presents itself during serious sickness. So I decided to do the only thing that made sense to me at the time. I just straight up told Garrett that I loved him.

And, to my great surprise, he loved me too. We didn't know how to make it work. But we just knew that we loved each other. And that seemed like enough for us.

Today, there's no question in my mind that Garrett is the best partner out there for me. Call him my soul mate if you want. I just call him my Garrett. There's nobody else for me—of that I'm sure. And I never would have known the greatest love of my life if I hadn't allowed myself, if I hadn't let go of my identity, if I hadn't been open to what came along.

We're here on Earth for a very short amount of time. We can decide to stick to a plan of the life we want, or we can decide to be open to the gifts that are coming in. The choice is ours. It's always been ours.

Detours Are More Fun Anyway

We're planners. As a society, we're planners. We decide what we're going to do with our lives when we turn eighteen. Either we head to college and declare a major, or we actually get out there in the real world. We have it all mapped out in our heads. We decide where we want to work, what we want to do, who we want to meet, when we want to get married, when the babies come along. We just feel more comfortable when we have a map.

In fact, this entire book started with a map—your own map of success on your own terms. We decided from the get-go exactly what success meant to us. We decided what we wanted success to look like, feel like, taste like, sound like—hell, even what it smelled like. We put together the most organized map we could possibly plan. We created a compass and a torch and everything else you'd need to go on this type of journey.

And now we're throwing it all out the window.

Anybody I know who's been successful in any way has veered off course. In fact, I think anybody I know, period—successful or not—has departed from the original blueprint.

Plans give us a great outline of where we want to go. But there comes a point when they just start holding us back. There comes a point when we start relying more on the plan than on the actual experience of living life. In the same way that other people's definitions of success trapped us before, our own definitions of success start trapping us now.

Things change. Circumstances shift. Life happens. We learn. We grow. We expand. We aren't the same person we were when we created the plan in the first place. That's the magic of the journey. It changes you. Actually, it makes you more of who you are. And then it's time to decide if you're going to stick so stubbornly to the plan you've had all along, or if you're going to take life in with each breath.

Success comes along when you least expect it. But only if you're willing to see it in whatever form it comes.

Our Past Is Not Our Identity

We make a series of choices in the past. We construct an idea of who we are based on our past thoughts, actions, and experiences. We think we know who we are now based on who we were—five minutes ago, six months ago, three years ago. But the truth is that we're constructing our identity anew every single moment. We don't live life in chunks of time; we live moment to moment. And that means that, each moment, you get to choose who you're going to be. That means that, each moment, you get to decide to follow the way you've been doing things or pick a new path. The past does not dictate the future. You've got a choice.

It's hard to know who you are. You think you've finally got it figured out. You've done the self-work, you've been to all the therapies, you've even done your affirmations. But then a strange urge comes up. Maybe you start liking chocolate ice cream instead of vanilla. Maybe you become an extrovert instead of an introvert. Maybe you're really creative and not into numbers anymore. And it makes you rethink everything you've known about yourself. It makes all of that self-work seem useless. It throws your lifelong beliefs for a loop.

Sounds frustrating. Sounds like it'd be a lot easier to just stick to the "you" that you know. Sounds like this random anomaly might come to pass, so there's no point in uprooting your life just to give in to a newfound preference.

But that's not how we work at all. The whole idea of identity is rooted in the assumption that we're constant beings. And, I don't know about you, but this guy's changing all the time.

We're elusive creatures. We think we've got our finger on it, and—*bam!*—we've changed again. We're always growing and evolving. In every moment, we learn something new, and that changes us forever. That's just part of life. And sticking to what you think you know—because it's easier—is directly impeding on that growth.

Success isn't something you just achieve and it's done. It isn't this consistent state of happiness. It's something you have to work toward every single day. It's a journey you have to commit yourself to. It's an understanding that you're a chaotic, ever-changing critter, and that's just part of the fun.

We decide to be successful in every moment. If we trip or fall or collapse, we always have another moment to choose success.

But we are not defined by our past; we are defined by the spontaneous decisions that we make in this moment. And the next. And the next.

Time to Play Hooky

We're good boys and girls. We do the right things. We try our best to be nice, follow the rules, eat well, do everything we're supposed to. But anyone who's ever dieted knows that the rules don't work 100 percent of the time. We need a cheat day. We need a little snack to keep us sane. Otherwise, we'll end up going off the deep end and binging on bad behavior. Otherwise, we'll wake up one day and realize that we've followed the rules all our lives—even if they're our own rules—and now we have to break them all. I think we call that a mid-life crisis.

We have to break out of the routine just to remind ourselves that we're alive. We have to skip work and head to the beach on a nice day, or sneak home early to surprise our love with some flowers, or—dare I say it—eat some chocolate cake on a bad day. We need to remind ourselves that a little chaos is good for our souls. That on-the-spot decisions remind us we always have a choice. That our intuition is a handy tool from time-to-time.

We've got it all wrong, and it's time to set the record straight. It's not that *some* rules are meant to be broken; it's that rules are meant to be broken *sometimes*. Every now and again, we've got to dig deep and pull out our own little rebel without a cause, just to remind ourselves that we can.

When we break free from the rules, we remind ourselves that we're empowered. That we have a choice. That we're in control of creating whatever kind of life we want.

We can divert from the path any time we want. We always have the choice of picking the thing that feels best in that moment, rather than the thing that we feel like we're supposed to do.

And, sometimes, we need to break the rules just to remind ourselves that we can.

The Thrill of a Road Trip

I've done a lot of road tripping in my day. In truth, I was a poor college student for many years, and I couldn't really afford a plane ticket. So I drove north to south and east to west, all over the country. It was just how I got places.

And I was always struck by the experience of driving there. Things never went as planned. We broke down, missed turns, took wrong exits. Sometimes we'd randomly stop somewhere that looked fun. We always ended up where we wanted to go eventually, but it never happened in the way we expected it to.

I learned to stop expecting at all on these road trips. Things just had a way of working themselves out. Truthfully, we had a way of coming up with last-minute solutions when shit hit the fan. And it always did at one point or another. But that wasn't something to prepare for and plan. That was just something to live. That was just part of the journey.

When I think back to all of my road trips, the most poignant memories happened in the car. They didn't happen at the destinations at all; they happened at the detours. They happened when we laughed about our psychotic-looking waiter, or during our made-up game of "Complete the Sentence." They happened when we created an entire song with backup vocals on the car ride home. They happened when we forgot to focus so intently on the plan that we got lost in the actual experience we were living.

The fun of a road trip is that it's a journey. We can make all the plans we want, but the journey is going to inevitably throw us for a loop. We're going to have urges to randomly stop for fried chicken or check out that used bookstore off the side of the road. And it's in those moments that we can decide to stick to the plan, or take the detour. It's in those moments that we can decide if we want to take the fastest route to the destination, or the path that feels the best right now. It's in those moments that we realize all we have is right now.

Success Never Looks Like
We Expected

When we start the journey to create success on our own terms, we have a rough idea of how it's supposed to look. We ignore anything on the path that doesn't match up to our sketch. We're people on a mission—we're determined to get successful. And we don't need any more distractions to stand in our way.

We all zip through the ten chapters before this one. We define success for ourselves, we conquer our fears, we get clear on our strengths, we find our passions. We keep cycling further and further into success on our own terms.

But you might notice that things don't look exactly as you expected. You might notice that the most successful parts of the journey aren't what you originally wanted at all. It just kind of appeared. And we have to decide if we're willing to go back on our word and try something we swore we'd never do, or if we keep surging forward, looking for the type of success we imagined.

A big part of success is being a hypocrite. It's going back on your word. It's swearing that you'd never write those cheesy list stories for a lot of social media shares, and then deciding that it's not so bad. It's thinking that hiring a cleaning lady is pretentious, until you realize it lets you spend quality time with your family. It's swearing off divorce until you're in the hot seat and realize that you're just holding yourself back from happiness. It's letting go of the image you had of success so you can accept the reality that's waiting for you.

Success is trying to get to us all the time. It's popping up in unexpected partnerships or forbidden love. It's hanging out at dinner parties and weekend getaways. It's been there all along, if you could just open your eyes and accept the opportunities being given to you.

Success requires risks. It requires you to take chances. It requires you to do things you never in a million years thought you'd be doing. Because, to be successful, we have to grow bigger than we already are. We have to give ourselves permission to allow success to find us. We have to be open to opportunities we never imagined.

Finding success isn't the hard part. It's accepting it that's the bitch. It might not come in the form we expected. It might not come wrapped with a pretty pink bow. But it's there. It's ours for the taking. If we can just be flexible enough to accept it. If we can just expand outside of our comfort zone and try something new.

If we can just decide to be successful and be open to whatever that means.

Challenges

Complete the following challenges before moving on to the next chapter. To allow yourself to be successful, you have to accept success in whatever form it comes. It may not look exactly as you expected, but that doesn't make it any less of a success.

1. Think over your biggest successes to date. Maybe you landed your dream job. Maybe romance fell right into your lap. You might have been featured in a newspaper. Or just made a huge sale. Think about exactly how it happened. Did everything go according to plan? Was it a straight and narrow path?

   Or did you feel like you diverted from the path to get there? You might have met a business contact on a plane ride. Or made a sale during a game of golf. Or met that reporter at a conference.

   Consider how often you've had success by going with the flow versus sticking to the plan.

2. Make a commitment to say "yes" to exciting opportunities this week. If anything catches your eye and gets you excited—regardless if you would normally do it or not—decide to say yes to it. You could see a networking event that sounds fun, or you might finally take your friend up on the offer to go skydiving. If any exciting opportunities come to you, even if they're outside your

normal rules of engagement, give yourself permission to say yes and accept whatever's coming in.

3. Decide to break the rules a little bit one day this week. Don't go rob a bank or torch your old office, but do something that reminds you that you're alive. Maybe you cheat and get yourself an ice cream cone on the walk home. Maybe you skip that boring meeting and head to the beach for the afternoon. Maybe you head to the airport and get on the cheapest flight spontaneously for a weekend getaway. Maybe you start dancing in the middle of the office. Whatever you choose to do, step outside of your rules, plan, and comfort zone to remind yourself that you can play hooky any time you want. You're always in control of your decisions. You're always in control of your life.

4. For the next month, make a decision to allow success to come in whatever form it appears. Instead of judging success by your own plan, decide to judge it by what feels good in the moment. If a partnership seems a little off topic, but just feels right to you, give it a shot. If you have a sudden urge to get published in your favorite blog, feel free to shoot them a note. If you have a secret crush on your co-worker, but he or she is totally not your type, give it a try. Oftentimes, success doesn't show up in the package we were expecting, but that doesn't make it any less successful. You just have to be willing to accept whatever comes along.

12

You've Already Reached Your Destination

When I started writing this book, I had to ask myself a lot of questions: What do I want to share with the world? What is *my* definition of success? And—most of all—am I really successful enough to write this book?

A kind of funny thing happens when you're forced to start living out the thing that you're supposedly an expert on. You start to see your life in a new way. You have to ask yourself the tough questions. You have to match up what you're practicing with what you're preaching.

We really are our worst clients. That will always be the case. And, regardless of the words I was writing, for the entire duration of the process, a little voice in the back of my head said, "Do you have enough money in your bank account to write a book on success? Maybe if you had another $50,000," or, "Do you have enough clients and blog readers to say you're successful? Maybe if you were completely overbooked with clients."

But I powered through. I quieted that little voice and just kept writing. My rational mind knew that the voice was just my fear of success. My rational mind knew that no amount of money or clients or fame would ever be enough for that voice. Unfortunately, our rational mind isn't always the easiest one to believe.

Then, one day, while taking a break from writing, I got up to dance. I dance all the time when I'm bored or tired or frustrated. It gets the creative juices flowing again. I just drop everything that I'm doing and I dance. Sometimes, I drag begrudging clients into it with me.

And, as I danced alone in my living room, while writing a book to help people find success, at 3:30 in the afternoon, in my dream apartment overlooking the skyline of my favorite city, I couldn't help but laugh. It started out as a snicker, then a chuckle, then a roaring laugh.

It didn't look like how I imagined. It wasn't the future I had dreamed of. But I knew that I was happy. So unbelievably, blissfully happy. If I couldn't accept how overwhelmingly successful I was at that very moment, then I'd never accept it.

It was the first moment that I really, really got it. It was the first moment that I really, truly understood success. And no little voice in the world had any power over me anymore.

Just moments later, Garrett, the love of my life, came bursting through the door with a curious expression on his face. "Why are you laughing?" he asked me.

"Because I'm successful," I said succinctly.

He looked me in the eyes with a soft smirk and said, "Of course you are. It's about time you realized it."

Success Happens When You Get There

There. We talk about it all the time. We allude to it like everybody knows what we're talking about. It's the mystical place that promises to make all of our problems go away.

When we get *there*, things will be different. When we get *there*, we'll be successful or happy or confident or smart or funny or cool. When we get *there*, we'll be enough. We'll be good enough or famous enough or rich enough. That's the place that makes everything get better. We just have to reach that destination, and the world will change.

We have this idea that if we get ourselves to some milestone in the race of life, we'll suddenly be transformed into who we want to be. We believe that losing weight will make us this confident, happy person. We believe that getting that promotion will finally make us successful. We believe that a new house or a fast car or a hot date will magically transform us into the person we're trying to become.

So we go on the journey. We fight our battles. We learn and change and grow. We take down obstacle after obstacle on our path to success. We get whatever it is we think we're looking for—the loads of customers or the high-profile news article. Maybe the ideal home or the fancy gadgets. Maybe free time or more money or the love of our life.

We finally make it *there*. The image in our head of what success is. The place that's supposed to magically transform us. The place that we believe stronger than anything will make us successful. And all we find on the top of that mountain is a mirror—a mirror reflecting back the image of ourselves.

We don't look any different. We don't feel any different. We don't seem to have changed in any real way. The fact of the matter is that we made it to exactly where we wanted to be. Not somebody else's definition of success—our definition of success. We did it right. We did everything right. And all we have to face is ourselves.

Success isn't some place outside of you. It isn't a certain salary or an expensive suit. It isn't the look of your living room, or the amount of free time you have in a day. It isn't even the relationships in your life or the quality of your work.

Success is a mindset. It's a way of looking at the world. It's the idea that you're already everywhere you'll ever be. That it doesn't matter where you are; it matters who you are. That you're happy with yourself and the life you lead. And the rest—well, that's just icing on the cake.

Assume This Is It

You never know what the future will hold. You may go on and one day become the next Oprah, or you may never have any more money or influence than you have right now. So why are you waiting to start living your dream life?

Go back over your original definition of success from the first exercise. What does it look like? How much free time do you have? How do you spend your days? What do your relationships look like? How do you allow people to treat you? What kinds of foods do you eat? How often do you exercise? How much fun is your life?

If you're waiting for your big break, you may be waiting a long time. You have to assume this is it. You have to assume you're as successful now as you're ever going to be. You may never have more money or more free time or a fancier house than you have right now. So how do you create a successful life with what you've got right now, instead of waiting to hit a certain metric?

Could you start eating the foods you said you'd eat when you're successful? Could you start setting the boundaries you want to set when you're successful? Could you start asking out the guys or gals you planned on approaching once you're successful? We have every opportunity to start treating ourselves as successes right now. We have every opportunity to start living the successful lives we've always dreamed of.

Maybe we have to sub in a Groupon-discounted massage for the fancy spa visit. And maybe we have to turn our dining room into Paris rather than jet set for a romantic evening. But we have the ability to live out our most successful fantasies right here, right now. If we aren't willing to afford ourselves success right now, we'll never be able to do it, no matter what particular milestone we reach.

This moment is all we know. This moment is all we have. It's now or never. We either decide to be successful with who we are and what we have today, or we decide to keep striving to achieve more. The decision to be successful or not is really up to us in the first place.

Nobody Will Ever Give You the Keys to Your Life

For all that we talk about success, the truth is that we're afraid of it. It's been sitting in front of us the entire time, just waiting to be claimed. But, instead of grabbing it right from the get-go, we're waiting around until somebody gives us permission. We're waiting for somebody to tell us that we deserve it and that it's okay to go after it.

We only start writing that novel after everyone in our lives tells us we're brilliant writers. We only ask for that raise after everyone tells us that we're underpaid. We wait to launch our own business until we've earned our way high enough up the ladder. We ask our friends to set us up with that cute guy or girl, rather than ask him or her out ourselves.

We're waiting for someone to give us permission to be successful because we don't think that we deserve it in the first place.

When I first started working by myself, I found every little way to trap myself. I wouldn't travel because I was making less money, despite a hefty savings account. I wouldn't go for midday walks because "someone might need me," so I chained myself to a desk. I resisted the urge to feel the full extent of my freedom because I didn't feel like I deserved it.

I thought, *Why should I get to spend my days the exact way I want to, while the rest of the world has to slave away at a nine to five?* The idea that I deserved freedom and success was so foreign to me that I was more comfortable making busy-work than I was with facing the prospect of having control over my life.

I was waiting for the day when someone would say to me, "Mike, you've been working so hard. Why don't you take an afternoon off?" or, "Mike, why don't you just raise your rates so you'll have the money you want?" Because I didn't feel that I had earned those privileges yet.

In every area of our lives, we're waiting for someone to hand over the keys. We make up excuses about who is controlling our lives because we're afraid of the power that comes with stepping up and taking control ourselves. We complain about our bosses and our clients and our mothers and our spouses. We swear that these people are making our lives miserable. In actuality, they're just the scapegoats. We're afraid to get as big as we really are, so we hold ourselves back in meaningless jobs or unhappy relationships or fake money woes.

The truth behind all of it is that we're just afraid to take the wheel and start driving. We're just afraid that if we really did exactly what we wanted all day, every day, we'd be successful—hugely, hugely successful. And we're not so sure we deserve that.

The real person standing in your way of success is you. It's been there, waiting for you, all this time. You've always had the keys to your life. Your hand has always been on the wheel, deciding to stay in that dead-end job or that toxic relationship. You've always been in control.

And it's a shame to see a Lamborghini stuck in that mess of traffic. It's time to shift into high gear. You were born to move, baby.

The Journey Is a Wild Goose Chase

The journey is over. We've reached the destination. But there isn't really a destination to reach. These steps—these phases of the journey—we're always cycling through them. We're always reaching deeper and deeper levels of success. Really, we're always reaching deeper and deeper levels of self-acceptance.

The truth—the little known secret that nobody wants to talk about—is that success doesn't have a ton to do with fancy marketing terms or revenue numbers. It doesn't have a ton to do with *The New York Times* cover stories and late-night parties. It's really about self-acceptance. It's really about happiness. It's really about being comfortable in your own skin. And no amount of market segmentation can ever really teach you that.

You've been able to reach success the whole time. You've always been enough to reach success. Good enough, smart enough, old enough, young enough, and everything else that you thought was holding you back. Who you are without that fancy title and that big-screen TV was always enough.

The joke's on you. I faked you out. I pulled a total Mr. Miyagi move here. Success is really about knowing who you are and accepting that. It's about recognizing that you have control to live the life you've always dreamed of, and you always have. It's about realizing that you're enough to change the world right now. It's about realizing that you already are changing the world.

This journey—this whole journey—was just a wild goose chase to get you to realize that. And, in today's world, we call that wild goose chase self-improvement.

Success Starts Now

I've read more motivational books than I can admit without blushing. My library is filled with self-help up the wazoo. And, as great as they are, the truth is that the books don't really mean a heck of a lot. They're incomplete. This book you have in your hands—the one I poured my heart and soul into—it's incomplete, too. It's just words on a page. Just somebody else's ramblings about building the life you've always been capable of building. It's not finished yet—not without your action.

If you're looking for a kick in the pants, here it is. This is your moment. Anything that's holding you back is just an excuse. You're just clinging on to old insecurities or meaningless fears or dark moments. There's no better time than right now to be successful.

You can walk away from this book a little inspired, maybe even a little amused. But, if you don't start taking action immediately, you're not completing this book here with me. You're stopping me from successfully accomplishing what I came here to do. And you know how I feel about people holding me back from success.

Take action. Do it right now. The second you close this book, do something. Anything. I don't care what it is. Just as long as you start moving.

We don't measure magnitude here; we measure direction. If you just take one step—no matter how tiny—every single day, at the end of the year, you'll be 365 times closer to accomplishing your dreams. All it takes is one step. Then another. And another. And, suddenly, you're walking straight into your dream life.

You've always been in control. You've always been able to. You've always been good enough.

So, enough already. It's time to be successful.

Challenges

Live the life you were meant to live. The one that's been waiting for you all along. The one that you are more than good enough to live.

Decide to be a success right now. And take a step forward.

ABOUT THE AUTHOR

Mike Iamele is a wellness coach, specializing in helping passionate, ambitious millennials overcome burnout and reclaim their definitions of success. He is a contributor to *MindBodyGreen, Lifehack, Under30CEO, YFS Magazine, Elephant Journal, and Brazen Life.* He holds a B.A. in Communication Studies and a Health Coaching Certification. He lives in Somerville, MA. Visit him at *www.bostonwellnesscoach.com.*

TO OUR READERS

Conari Press, an imprint of Red Wheel/Weiser, publishes books on topics ranging from spirituality, personal growth, and relationships to women's issues, parenting, and social issues. Our mission is to publish quality books that will make a difference in people's lives—how we feel about ourselves and how we relate to one another. We value integrity, compassion, and receptivity, both in the books we publish and in the way we do business.

Our readers are our most important resource, and we appreciate your input, suggestions, and ideas about what you would like to see published.

Visit our website at *www.redwheelweiser.com* to learn about our upcoming books and free downloads, and be sure to go to *www.redwheelweiser.com/newsletter* to sign up for newsletters and exclusive offers.